EYEWITNESSES

EYEWITNESSES

Biblical Foundations in Christian Spirituality

—General Editor: Fr. John Horn, S.J.—

Associate Editors:
Seminarians • First Year Theology •
St. Vincent De Paul Regional Seminary

⊗ ENROUTE

En Route Books & Media
5705 Rhodes Avenue, St. Louis, MO 63109
Contact us at contactus@enroutebooksandmedia.com
© En Route Books & Media, 2017

Cover design by TJ Burdick
Format Editor, Thomas Pulickal
Cover image credit: Graphicstock.com

Interior image credits:
Christ on the Storm, https://commons.wikimedia.org/wiki/
File:Rembrandt_Christ_in_the_Storm_on_the_Lake_of_
Galilee.jpg

https://commons.wikimedia.org/wiki/File:Gebhard_Fugel_
Moses_vor_dem_brennenden_Dornbusch_c1920.jpg

Smiling Crucified Jesus, Courtesy of Franca Salvo A.O.

The Resurrection of Christ, https://commons.wikimedia.
org/wiki/File:Jacopo_Tintoretto_-_The_Resurrection_of_
Christ_-_WGA22476.jpg

Return of the Prodigal Son, https://upload.wikimedia.org/
wikipedia/commons/thumb/9/93/Rembrandt_Harmensz_van_
Rijn_-_Return_of_the_Prodigal_Son_-_Google_Art_Project.
jpg/785px-Rembrandt_Harmensz_van_Rijn_-_Return_of_the_
Prodigal_Son_-_Google_Art_Project.jpg

Paperback ISBN: 978-1-950108-60-2
E-book ISBN: 978-1-63337-160-6
LCCN: 2017933821

Printed in the United States of America

"Mission Bethlehem" in Wharf Jeremie, Haiti, will be the recipient of all royalties received from book sales. This is a Catholic community of missionaries who live with the poor in the same situation as they live. The missionaries work with those who live on the streets and suffer from various addictions, inviting them into a house of hospitality that provides support to them in their choice to leave their vices. In engaging in this kind of work, the missionary community desires to live as an image of the Holy Family inspired by the love of St. Joseph and Mary with Jesus. Mission Bethlehem also sponsors a school for children, a clinic for those suffering from physical and spiritual malnutrition and an orphanage.

See the postscript at the end of this book for photos and more information.

As Rector of St. Vincent de Paul Regional Seminary, I am very proud of our students for pulling together to publish this little work. Each topic is quite evidently the fruit of their study and prayer. I believe any reader will be edified and encouraged on their own faith journey by the insights and personal reflections contained in this book.

– Msgr. David L. Toups, S.T.D., President-Rector
of St. Vincent de Paul Regional Seminary,
Boynton Beach, Florida

Eyewitnesses provides a wonderful summary of foundational Biblical themes illustrated through personal examples. The simple format nourishes the reader while inviting the reader's personal response.

– Fr. Rich Gabuzda, Executive Director,
Institute of Priestly Formation

The students' testimonies in first year theology are expressions not only of dogmatic faith but also of personal faith. The reflection questions at the end of each chapter help guide readers to personalize their faith by leading them to a conversion of heart. This is a necessary process of growth in head, heart and hands as taught by Pope Francis.

– Fr. Jack Hunthausen, SJ, Spiritual Director
and Pastoral Ministry

Eyewitnesses is a most edifying testament to the personal verification of truth that is indispensable for all disciples of Jesus, but especially for those called to serve the unfolding of faith of their brothers and sisters as future priests. I am impressed and encouraged by the unique inspiration that this project represents and by the way in which these reflections manifest authentic encounters with the Risen One whose beauty saves and whose gentleness heals.

– Fr. Peter J. Williams, Vice Rector for Formation, St. Paul Seminary School of Divinity at the University of St. Thomas

These essays and reflective questions lift the veil, revealing the glory of God coming closer as Psalm 42:7 expresses, "deep calls to deep." May you enter into the deep waters of new life through these Eyewitnesses.

– Mrs. Jane Guenther, Director of Catholic Renewal Center, Archdiocese of St. Louis, Missouri

Dedicated to St. Joseph—the first eyewitness to Jesus and Mary's love!

CONTENTS

Foreword

James Keating, Ph.D.

To suffer the coming of God is the crux of seminary formation. To suffer God is simply a way of saying that in His presence one undergoes a movement from the sins and habits I now love to the actions and thoughts which Christ loves. These sins and superficialities are replaced by the substance of loving what truly ennobles each of us, fascination with God. Without a fascination with God who is Beauty, a man loses interest in prayer and even love.

This is true because beauty carries us into union with God. Without beauty a person becomes fixated on "taking" from reality rather than "receiving" from it. To be affected by the beauty of Christ, to receive His person, such is the way to becoming a giving person. Beholding the beauty which is Christ, contemplating Him, is the "river in the wasteland," the source of life among the life-ebbing involvement in distractions which possesses so many today. The remedy is depth; the remedy is to contemplate life and love—not death, not isolation. Faith makes it clear that if we are to ascend from superficial immediacy to deep liberty, we must move from only thinking about Christ to holding Him in our being. This is the way of contemplation.

To contemplate the beauty of the Crucified is to place oneself in a condition of emotional vulnerability, aware of one's longing to be acted upon in love, healed, and liberated. In the presence of God's Beauty, we want to become a new creation. Much of the popular culture today is enamored with the "fantasy" industry, one built upon loneliness and alienation dragging at the depths of every man. To reverse this "drag," we encourage the seminarian to place himself in a position to contemplate God so that he will come to know the way of freedom for us all, and show us the way there.

The essays in this book reflect the radical conversion their authors are undergoing in the seminary. There is no other place in the Western education system that is as committed to the conversion of the whole person as is the Catholic seminary. What you have before you in these essays is the budding fruit of such conversions. Even at this early stage of seminary formation you can feel the freedom that is reaching these authors as they come to breathe the oxygen of prayer and truth more deeply.

If we prayerfully read these witness essays we too can begin to think about leaving the superficialities of culture behind and begin to gather around Christ, as these authors are now

11

doing, and learn from Him. Allow these essays to heal you as you read them and say a prayer for the seminaries of the world as they endeavor to gift it with the kind of men we most desperately need today; free men in Christ. Men not bound to the superficiality of western popular culture but bound only to the beauty which emanates from Christ, Truth itself.

Deacon James Keating, Ph.D.
Institute for Priestly Formation
Creighton University, Nebraska

INTRODUCTION

Fr. John Horn, S.J.

The impelling desire and reason for this small catechetical book is illuminated beautifully by these words from Pope Francis:

> On the lips of the catechist the first proclamation must ring out over and over: "Jesus Christ loves you; he gave his life to save you; and now he is living at your side every day to enlighten, strengthen and free you." This first proclamation is called "first" not because it exists at the beginning and then can be forgotten or replaced by other more important things. It is first in a qualitative sense because it is the principal proclamation, the one which we must hear again and again in different ways, the one which we must announce one way or another throughout the process of catechesis, at every level at every moment. (*The Joy of the Gospel* #126)

This is a collection of essays written by my class of diocesan seminarians and a young lay woman who are all in their first year of Theological study at St. Vincent De Paul Regional Seminary in Florida. These essays represent a selection of basic topics of interest in Christian Spirituality. In each essay a brief teaching in Biblical Theology is excised from Fr. Xavier Léon-Dufour's seminal work, the *Dictionary of Biblical Theology*. The quotes from Fr. Dufour provide a window into foundational truths that are alive in Sacred Scripture. Following any quotation from Fr. Dufour's work a simple page number is listed. Each essay also contains a humble attempt to speak to what Pope Francis refers to as the "first proclamation." Through our "eyewitness accounts" of what we have tasted and seen with our own eyes, what we have heard concerning the Word of life—we now desire to proclaim to you so that you might have fellowship with us. Our fellowship is with the Father and with His Son, Jesus Christ. We offer this collection of testimonies so that your joy may be more complete (1 Jn. 1:1-4). I am indebted to seminarian Thomas Pulickal for his charity and generosity. His assistance in orchestrating the design of this work was a great gift.

Because images speak and think within us, the essays are sometimes accompanied by a work of art that serves to engage your imagination. We hope that the images selected by each student will assist in unveiling some of the mystery of the foundational Biblical truths and the personal testimonies. The images serve as a partial inspired synthesis of what the essay teaches. Two reflection questions are also provided following each essay. These help to bridge the teachings with your own life of faith.

As you read these stories, illustrating the meaning of several Biblical foundations in Christian Spirituality, it is our hope that your heart will be stirred to seek Jesus' risen presence at work in the events of daily life. We write to build up our fellowship in Jesus' risen presence.

Serving as the teacher-mentor for these students has strengthened greatly the gift of faith in my own heart. I am immensely grateful for the generosity of these students-seminarians. Is there a more important or more beautiful gift? Pope Benedict at World Youth Day in Australia said, "There is nothing more beautiful than being surprised by the Gospel, by the encounter with Christ... And, we know that there is nothing more beautiful than to know Him and to speak to others of our friendship with Him."

Amid life's trials testimonies release faith and hope. I pray that you receive blessings as you read. May you be captivated anew by faith and hope to know how you are the object of the fullness of Jesus' affection and love!

FAITH

Anonymous

For the Bible faith is the source and center
of all religious life (162).

Introduction

Faith, the center of our very existence, is a gift from God.
As a gift, we rely on the Giver of the gift in order to receive and
grow in faith. I am drawn to this understanding of the origin of
faith and its entire purpose as *relationship*. This relationship
through faith is the center of all life. Understanding the importance of faith as relationship (rather than an obligation) pulls
us back from a "faith" that feels abstract, seems impersonal,
and becomes a heavy burden. The prologue of the Gospel of
John tells us that the Word became flesh in the Person of Jesus
Christ and dwelt among us. When we understand this as in the
depth of our being, faith can no longer be seen as a mechanical

series of external actions (following the right rules) to achieve a desired result (heaven). Instead, we are invited to see faith as a gift from God which orients us toward deeper union with the giver of the gift.

I will examine two questions throughout the definitions of faith presented in the *Dictionary of Biblical Theology*: Where does the gift of faith come from? What is the purpose or object of the gift of faith? In regards to the first question: Faith cannot be generated at will from within, but rather is a gift from God. Therefore, God is the source of the gift of faith which allows us to encounter the Word made flesh. In regards to the second question: God became man and dwelt among us to draw humanity into a deeper relationship with Himself. Reception of this gift allows the believer to receive an abundant life and have it to the fullest degree.

Where does faith come from?

Man cannot generate the beginning of faith or its depth; man relies on God who is the source of the gift of faith. As Jesus performed signs and wonders, He drew large crowds to Himself and once asked the disciples, "Who do people say that the Son of Man is?" It was Peter who, on behalf of the other disciples, gave the right answer: "You are the Messiah, the Son of the living God." From where did Peter have the ability to recognize the Word made flesh in his midst? Jesus affirms Peter saying, "Blessed are you, Simon son of Jonah. For flesh and blood has not revealed this to you, but my heavenly Father" (Matt 16:13-20). Peter was not guessing, he was not grasping, he *knew* in the depths of his being that the Person standing before him was the Christ. It was God Himself who gave that gift of faith to Peter, which allowed Peter to peer beyond what was immediately evident to his senses.

Some might ask the question, "But what of me today? Can I believe just as the disciples who walked with Jesus two thousand years ago?" In short, yes you can believe just as the disciples did in their time! The gift of faith is not reserved only for those who literally walked with Jesus and saw Him face to face. Faith is not contingent upon a constant reception of miracles and signs, but upon an ongoing spiritual encounter with the One we love. Man could never, by his own strength or will, peer beyond what immediately appears to his senses. Faith comes from the Holy Spirit, a gift which can be received or rejected, and "to those who did accept him he gave power to become children of God, to those who believe in his name" (John 1:12). To realize that faith itself is a gift frees us from the burden of belief that we are the source of faith or that we can grasp at faith to deepen our relationship with God. God already offers us the gift of faith and it is for us to receive or reject the gift. Even today, our faith is valid because of the God who has come among us, whom we have encountered, and who proclaims to the depths of our heart: "Blessed are those who have not seen and have believed" (John: 20:29). Thus, God is the source of the gift of faith, allowing us to recognize and enter into relationship with the One who said, "Once I was dead, but now I live forever and ever" (Rev 1:18).

What is the purpose or object of faith?

Having received the gift of faith through the Word made flesh, we now turn our gaze toward the purpose of faith: a deeper relationship with God. One might ask the question, "Why have I received the gift of faith?" God, a Triune relationship of Persons, freely created from nothing all that we see, all that we experience, and our very lives. Unity with God is the reason God became man; so that man might share in the unitive love of the Father, Son and Holy Spirit. We need not remain in uncertainty why God became man. Jesus Himself tells us the reason as He proclaims, "I came so that they might have life and have it more abundantly" (John 10:10). God, in His infinite love and mercy, has willed us for our own sake. We can add nothing to the greatness of God. We cannot perform in a way that impresses the Father. This point frees us from an understanding of faith as an obligation, allowing us to see beyond what immediately appears to the truth of who we are: the children of God (John 1:12). As children of God, we patiently await the day when "we shall see Him as He is" and enter into the fullness of relationship with Him in heaven (1 John 3:2).

A Personal Witness

Faith in Jesus Christ has irrevocably changed my life. When I was younger, faith seemed like a mechanical series of rules to follow to gain heaven after death. In my understanding, I was missing something crucial: relationship. This change within my heart did not happen overnight or in one moment. In fact, I sometimes slip back into an understanding of faith as an obligation. One example immediately came to my heart to illustrate the change in my understanding of faith. When I arrived at St. Vincent de Paul Regional Seminary I was struck by the peace I felt as I drove onto the campus. Being a seminarian feels very counter-cultural, but as I arrived here I felt as if there was no other place on earth I was supposed to be. Only faith makes this possible. Without the gift of faith, my former career as mortgage banker seems more grounded, more rational, closer to the "right thing to do." Something has changed within my heart since coming to seminary. In faith, I can peer beyond "the right thing to do" according to society, and rely completely upon God. Through faith, I can receive the Body and Blood of Jesus Christ every day even though my senses only experience ordinary bread and wine. Having received the gift of faith, I can say, "Amen, I believe" to all that the Church believes and professes. How could I ever turn away from the One who created me for relationship? How could I ever refuse the gift?

Conclusion

The staggering doctrine of the Incarnation, that God became man and dwelt among us, is the source of our fidelity and the object of our desire. Faith is not an obligation, nor is faith sustained by a static memory of God. Faith is a gift sustained by a dynamic and living relationship with the giver of the gift of faith, God Himself. Rooted in this understanding, the believer can recognize the gift of faith as the source and center of his or her existence and, with joyful anticipation, await the day when "we shall see Him as He is" (1 John 3:2).

—Reflection Questions—

1. How have you encountered Jesus Christ in daily life and in what ways has your faith grown as a result of that encounter?
2. In what ways is God calling you into a deeper relationship of faith with Him?

THE HEART

Thomas Pulickal

*All they can do is 'rend their heart' (Jl 2:13) and
present themselves before God with a "broken and
contrite heart" (Ps 51:19) to beg their Lord to
"create in them a clean heart" (228).*

"A broken and contrite heart, O God, you will not despise" (Ps 51:19 RSV-CE). These words from Psalm 51 represent to us the hopeful prayer of David, a man who had committed a grave sin and was deeply repentant of it. These words
capture his hope and even his confidence that God would forgive him; that no matter how great the sin, God mercifully accepts everyone who comes to Him with "a broken and contrite
heart." While we can and should relate to David's prayer when
we find ourselves concretely in a similar situation, we can also
relate to these inspired words as we find ourselves everyday,
on a more existential level. In light of a deep-seated rebellion

within our hearts, a rebellion visibly manifested throughout the history of Israel, our many self-powered strivings for the Good must finally collapse (and keep collapsing) into a foundational disposition of humility and contrition of heart. This collapsing marks the end of a man being his own savior, the death of the old man who, being under the demands of the Law, is also under the Law's curse (c.f. Rom 6). And from this dying, from this broken heart of humility and contrition, faith and confidence in God mysteriously springs forth as new life. This is a total transformation of the human heart, but it is not a work of human excellence, since "for man it is impossible" (Matt 19:26 RSV-CE). Rather, it is the initiative of God who, moved with compassion for His people, promised, "I will give you a new heart" (Ezek 36:26 RSV-CE), a promise He fulfills through the Incarnation and Resurrection of Jesus Christ.

Contrary to how we are often accustomed to living, it is more important for us to undergo a transformation of the heart than it is to improve in skills, appearances, confidence, experience, or knowledge, though these are all important in a secondary sense. While we cannot transform our own heart, we can strive to come before God with our hearts broken and contrite, which is the disposition most conducive to receiving the new heart that God promises.

What do we mean by heart?

To properly understand the significance of the Biblical phrase "broken and contrite of heart," especially to understand it as a foundational disposition for life and formation, we must examine the Biblical sense of the word "heart." The Catechism of the Catholic Church states: "But in naming the source of prayer, Scripture speaks sometimes of the soul or the spirit, but most often of the heart (more than a thousand times)" (CCC 2562).

In a phrase such as "the heart of the city," heart refers to the very center, which is not necessarily spatially the center but the place within the city that most truly makes the city the very city that it is known to be. In other words, while the whole geographical region is the city, some specific area within it gives it its defining characteristic. Similarly, in the human person, the heart has always been used to capture a specifically inner place in the human person, which is the defining place. While both the Biblical and modern senses of the word heart express something inner to man, the significant difference is that the modern usage only pertains to a limited aspect of man's interiority; whereas in the Bible, its meaning is much more inclusive and integrated.

The heart in our culture is a symbol almost exclusively of the affective life of man, which is nearly the only meaning conveyed by the word in modern language. Phrases such as "it touched my heart" or "my heart is breaking" convey a vivid image to us today. The Biblical word does not neglect this signification. For example, we find texts such as "Thou hast given him his heart's desire" (Ps 21:3 RSV-CE) and "you shall cry out for pain of heart" (Isa 65:14 RSV-CE). On the other hand, the word heart in Hebrew encompasses far more than just affectivity, since it signifies the whole inner life of man, including feelings, plans, memories, decisions, and ideas. This difference in meaning makes certain phrases in Scripture sound unusual to us. A very clear example is found in Sirach 17:6. The RSV-CE translates this verse as, "He made for them tongue and eyes; he gave them ears and a mind for thinking." Nearly every translation is similar. But literally translated, the last few words would be not "a mind for thinking," but "a *heart* for thinking." The heart can indeed be the place of thinking because for the Hebrew the heart of man is the center of man, similar to the sense in which we speak of the heart of a city. The heart is the center of a person that is most truly that person, in contrast, for example, to his mere appearances. Understood this way, it is clear why "to think" belongs to man's heart, just as much as feeling, deciding, or recollecting. In Scripture, the heart is the deep place within a person where he can even be in dialog with himself (c.f. Gen 17:17, Deut 7:17). Thus, " a broken and contrite heart" is not limited to a set of affective experiences but can truly represent a foundational disposition that affects all the areas of our inner life.

How external practices can go wrong

As we have seen, the Biblical image of the heart is a far more integrated one, incorporating the whole of the inner life of man. This, however, raises the question of what is *not* included in the heart. In a very general way, one can say that if the heart represents the center or the inner core of the person, it is meant to exclude or de-emphasize all the "outer" aspects of human life. This divide between the heart and the outer aspects may seem like a disintegrated approach to examining the human person, and indeed in some sense it is. The disintegration of inner and outer is not properly human (i.e. it is not natural to man in God's original design), but it is nevertheless a notable characteristic of fallen humanity.

Normally, a person's actions (Luke 6:44), his facial expressions (Sir 13:25), and his words (Prov 16:23), in different degrees, communicate his very heart. The book of Sirach states, "A cheerful face indicates a heart full of good" (Sir 13:25 RSV-CE). Innumerable experiences of our own can confirm this, such as seeing the cheerful face of a humble religious sister, and thereby in some way experiencing her holiness. At the same time many of our experiences have also contradicted this outright. The fact that outward behaviors and expressions can communicate the heart, also gives an avenue for deception or even just being "fake." One can fool others into believing that one has a good heart or has good intentions by imitating the expressions, behaviors, and words that would naturally express a good heart. Once the deception is discovered by the other this leads to a terrible collapse of trust, in a specific way to that relationship but often also in a broader way concerning the trustworthiness of human beings in general. Thus, the sinfulness of man involves the disintegration of his inner self (his intentions, thoughts, sentiments, etc.) and his outward behavior. As we shall see, this becomes particularly evident in the history of the Israelites, and a specific problem that the Lord addresses through the prophets.

The desperation and salvation of Israel

Because they were the Chosen People of God, the Israelites had the richest religious patrimony with beautiful prayers, symbols, rituals, sacred texts, the Ten Commandments, and much more. Moses, well aware of this, spoke to the Israelites in this way:

> For ask now of the days that are past, which were before you, since the day that God created man upon the earth, and ask from one end of heaven to the other, whether such a great thing as this has ever happened or was ever heard of. Did any people ever hear the voice of a god speaking out of the midst of the fire, as you have heard, and still live? Or has

27

any god ever attempted to go and take a nation for himself from the midst of another nation, by trials, by signs, by wonders, and by war, by a mighty hand and an outstretched arm, and by great terrors, according to all that the LORD your God did for you in Egypt before your eyes? To you it was shown, that you might know that the LORD is God; there is no other besides him (Deut 4:32-35 RSV-CE).

And yet, the Israelites strayed from God time and again. Even though they often maintained the religious rituals, prayers, and observances, the Lord was not pleased with them because their hearts were not genuine. Thus, we find in Scripture many instances where the Lord rebukes them for their duplicity and calls them to conversion of heart. One of the most direct and succinct instances of this is when, through the prophet Joel, the Lord says, "Rend your heart, not your garments" (Joel 2:13 RSV-CE). In the Hebrew tradition, the tearing of one's garments was an expression of deep, heart-felt contrition at having offended God (Josh 7:6). But even this began to be performed merely externally, no longer as an authentic expression of true sorrow for one's sins. It is as though the Israelites felt that they could fool God, just as one man fools another, by doing all the external things that they ought to have done, while concealing the corruption of their heart. Of course, this was futile, since "the LORD sees not as man sees;

man looks on the outward appearance, but the LORD looks on the heart" (1 Sam 16:7 RSV-CE).

Therefore, the Lord rejected the worship of the Israelites. He rejected their feasts and solemnities, saying, "I hate, I despise your feasts, and I take no delight in your solemn assemblies." He rejected their public worship: "Even though you offer me your burnt offerings and cereal offerings, I will not accept them, and the peace offerings of your fatted beasts I will not look upon." He rejected their hymns and rich, liturgical music: "Take away from me the noise of your songs; to the melody of your harps I will not listen." For what the Lord desired was righteousness (Amos 5:21-24 RSV-CE).

If the heart of a person is corrupt, there does not appear to be much hope for him in himself. Whatever actions he does, whatever words he says, or whatever rituals he observes, all of these will be tarnished by his inner corruption. As Jesus taught, "Are grapes gathered from thorns, or figs from thistles? So, every sound tree bears good fruit, but the bad tree bears evil fruit" (Matt 7:16-17 RSV-CE). Because of the proliferation of sin, the Israelites, and indeed the whole human race, found themselves with a deep-seated rebellion against God that was not just in their behaviors, but in the very core of their beings, i.e. in their heart, and none of their outward actions could offer any hope of salvation. Thus the Lord pronounced His truthful judgment, "This people has a stubborn and rebellious heart" (Jer 5:23 RSV-CE).

In light of all this, we can understand the tremendous significance of the hopeful prayer of the repentant Psalmist. It is impossible to bypass the reality of our rebellious heart by mere externals or by pretending to be righteous. For as Scripture says, "They have all gone astray, they are all alike corrupt; there is none that does good, no, not one" (Ps 14:3 RSV-CE). But since David was "a man after God's own heart" (1 Sam 13:14 RSV-CE) and knew of "the depths of [His] compassion" (Ps 51:1 RSV-CE), he had confidence through hope that the Lord would have mercy on him, on a sinner who repents. Thus, rather than pretending to be good and self-standing, he approached God through the doorway of His mercy, with a broken and contrite heart, and his prayer was not rejected.

Seeing the rebellious heart of man and his hopelessness in himself, the Lord God, full of compassion, made an incredible promise through the prophet Ezekiel. "I will sprinkle clean water upon you, and you shall be clean from all your uncleannesses, and from all your idols I will cleanse you. A new heart I will give you, and a new spirit I will put within you; and I will take out of your flesh the heart of stone and give you a heart of flesh" (Ezek 36:25-26 RSV-CE). By this prophecy, the Lord announced that He Himself would accomplish in man that which he could not accomplish on his own. This prophecy was fulfilled in Jesus. Through His Incarnation, Death, and Resurrection, Christ took upon Himself the human heart with all its rebelliousness against God and He transformed it from within, offering us a new heart in His heart.

A Personal Witness

This year was my first year living in a seminary. Naturally, the first week was a bit of a transition for me. I was already used to the structure and order of each day having lived in a community house for a few years, but I experienced a troubling feeling that we were all being watched, that in this enclosure of one hundred men in formation, every social interaction or every gesture in prayer was being noted and evaluated. This feeling accompanied me everywhere, even in my times of private prayer, and even once or twice into my dreams!

Needless to say, this feeling was stifling to my spirit, and it was certainly not conducive to feeling at home in what would be my new home for the next several years. But the Lord always has a way of breaking through. It was actually only during a five day silent retreat that we had during the second week that I even became fully aware of my uneasiness. I brought it to the Lord and to my retreat spiritual director. The Lord gave me one clear passage from Scripture that literally changed the course of everything.

> You blind Pharisee! first cleanse the inside of the cup and of the plate, that the outside also may be clean (Matt 23:26 RSV-CE).

There I was, worrying about my appearance and gestures and the way I was being perceived or evaluated; whereas the

Lord was looking to my heart. He could not have been more direct. *"First* cleanse the inside…*that* the outside also may be clean." He was not saying that the outsides do not matter. But he was saying that the outsides (1) are only a far second in importance as compared to the transformation of the heart, and (2) the change of heart comes *first* so that the outsides may reflect what is first of all in the heart.

Through this experience with the Lord in prayer, I began to recall how intimate our relationship had been: from heart to Heart, from this broken heart to a Heart of infinite tenderness. The Lord was calling me back into the more authentic dimensions of our relationship and also of life. I asked myself, "What good would it be for the world if I merely learned all the best mannerisms and appearances and skills? Do we not already have politicians for that? And they are far better at it anyway." Indeed as Christians, we must be people of the heart. For "the LORD sees not as man sees; man looks on the outward appearance, but the LORD looks on the heart" (1 Sam 16:7 RSV-CE).

Conclusion

As Scripture makes perfectly evident and as it challenges us, I believe that nothing remains but for us to abandon our many pretensions, our self-sufficiency and self-righteousness, and to approach God like David—through the doorway of His mercy with broken and contrite hearts. In the gaze of His merciful compassion, we can have confidence that He will bestow upon us the new hearts that He promised through Ezekiel. This complete transformation of the heart is the formation that the Lord wishes for us over and above every kind of externalized self-improvement or social advancement, and He alone is capable of accomplishing it.

> **I have promised, and I will do it, says the LORD** (Ezek 37:14 RSV-CE).

—Reflection Questions—

1. What images of myself do I tend to project on to God before I allow Him to love me, knowing that He only seeks a humble contrite heart?

2. Imagine the beauty of the new heart that the Lord desires to give us. What would my life look like *today* if I lived according to this new heart?

PRAYER

Simi Sahu

*God of mercy, when it is hard for us to trust in you,
why should we worry? Being in your presence in a
peaceful silence is already praying. And you understand all that we are. Even a sigh can be a prayer.*

~ Brother Roger of Taizé

Most descriptions of prayer by holy men and women of
our faith use the simplest gestures and words such as "a sigh," "a
cry" or "a simple look turned toward heaven."[1] Even so, prayer
remains a mystery to believers, causing us to ask with the disciples, "Lord teach us to pray" (Luke 11:1). A life of prayer is a
life spent *learning* to pray, again and again, from those who pray
deeply, from scriptures and from Jesus Himself. This journey can
be helped by knowing prayer to be real, intimate and transforma-

---

1   Thérèse of Lisieux, *Story of a Soul*, third edition (Washing-
ton, DC: ICS Publications, 2013), ch. 10.

tive. Each of these elements comes with its own struggle and hope which are explored below.

Prayer is Real

And he came to the disciples and found them sleeping; and he said to Peter, "So, could you not watch with me one hour?"

~Matt 26:40

The disciples had known Jesus to pray frequently and deeply. They had witnessed Him withdrawing from the crowds to pray (Matt 14:13), performing miracles with prayer (John 6:11), and even saw Moses and Elijah when they joined Him (Luke 9:28-30). Still, when He asked them to pray in the final hours before His passion, left to themselves, they could not help but fall asleep. We too are often unable to stay "awake" in prayer, perhaps because it is not as *real* to us as it was to Jesus. Prayer can easily become a primarily verbal or intellectual exercise, far removed from our hearts.

The Catechism of the Catholic Church exhorts us to pray from the heart which is "the place of encounter" and "our hidden center" (CCC 2563). The heart is our authentic self, in quest of the true good (446), which is God Himself. Thus keeping our hearts apart from our prayer can starve both the heart and the prayer, each languishing for the other. Our hearts can shy away from prayer due to a lack of faith which doubts if God is truly listening. To this, Jesus assures us that the Father sees, knows and acts in the "secret" (Matt 6:6) of our hearts.

We are further encouraged by the confident prayer of the prophets and kings in the history of Israel (445) and of Jesus (447-8), especially in times of great trial and pain. This prayer was not personal time taken to calm down or "educate" others; rather, it affected history and their actions in a decisive way. Confidence in and from God enabled Israel to march toward the Red Sea with the Egyptians on their backs, and the Maccabees to always pray before going into battle. Jesus' mission and prayer could not be separated one from the other as seen in His prayer before He called the disciples to Himself, hours before the Passion and on the Cross, moments before His death.

Prayer is Intimate

Then he said to Thomas, "Put your finger here, and see my hands; and put out your hand, and place it in my side; do not be faithless, but believing." Thomas answered him, "My Lord and my God!"

~John 20:27-28

Thomas loved Jesus, had forsaken his family and work for His sake, and even exhorted the other disciples, saying, "Let us also go, that we may die with Him" (John 11:16). He was not lying. Thomas remained with Jesus, even as many others abandoned Him (John 6:66-69). Yet, after seemingly being left by Jesus who gave Himself up to His enemies and died on the Cross, Thomas grew indignant. When the other disciples were overcome with joy after seeing the Risen Christ, Thomas responded with the cold words, "Unless I see… I will not believe" (John 20:25). We too, after years of following Jesus, have boundaries beyond which He is not allowed. We too, like Thomas, find our hearts to be "deceitful" (228), abandoning the One we love despite our best efforts, our most fervent promises.

In reality, these unexpected retreats that our hearts make are evidence that God repeatedly takes initiative to come close to us. His closeness can be intimidating since it "lays bare the stains of the creature, its nothingness, its radical weakness" (203). But we must try, again and again, to remain open and vulnerable before God, calling to mind "what love the Father has given us, that we should be called children of God; and so we are" (1 John 3:1). Our fears melt away slowly as we recognize that "sonship is at the heart of prayer" (449), which means this relationship is not founded upon our own righteousness but God's initiative. In this intimate space we are drawn deeper into God's own heart and recognize that prayer "does not at all mean to ask only for the things of heaven, but rather to want what Jesus wants" (448).

Prayer is Transformative

Jesus said to her, "I who speak to you am he." So the woman left her water jar, and went away into the city, and said to the people, "Come, see a man who told me all that I ever did. Can this be the Christ?"

~John 4:26, 28-29

The "woman at the well" went there at a time when she would encounter fewer people, presumably because of her colorful past. However, while encountering Christ she was not repulsed by the mention of her sins. She even ran to help the very people she was scared of a little while before. This change was neither magical nor one forced by an iron will. The change came from a transformation of who she was, what she now knew of God and what she understood about herself. Her actions were not one of a puppet dominated by a micromanaging puppeteer, but rather of a heart in love, in union with Jesus.

To be in union with Jesus is to walk in His commandments. Unlike the seemingly instant transformation of the woman at the well, it takes most of us many tries over the years to learn to walk in this way. So we remain in prayer, which "enlarges our desires until it receives God's desire of us. In prayer we grow big enough to house God's desire in us which is the Holy Spirit."[2] We find that the Holy Spirit "helps us in our

---

2   Ann Ulanov and Barry Ulanov, *Primary Speech: A Psychology of Prayer* (Westminster: John Knox Press, 1982), 9.

weakness" (Rom 8:26) since God's power "does not triumph to destroy, but to purify and to regenerate" (203) us.

Finally, it is important to mention that the transformation we undergo through prayer is not one that estranges us from ourselves, but rather helps us to become who we truly are: made in the image and likeness of God (Gen 1:27). The works that we do as transformed men and women bear witness to God's creative power and our own distinct dignity. Far from holding us back in any way, God desires for us to share in His great work and do even greater things (John 14:1). Since we are His creation and by adoption His sons, we freely trust that no one, even we ourselves, is more interested in helping us become our truest, most beautiful selves than God.

> *Blessed are the men whose strength is in you, in*
> *whose heart are the highways to Zion.*
>
> ~Psalm 84:5

A Personal Witness

I especially experienced how real, intimate and transformative prayer is in the process of explaining my desire to discern the call to consecrated life to a family member. Being from a different faith tradition, he found it very difficult to understand the validity and value of the call to holy virginity. My first instinct was to explain to him in a clear and logical manner the origins and history of this beautiful vocation. However, in prayer I felt the Lord asking me to remain silent, and let Him speak for me. Given my nature and how our relationship was strongly affected by this, I was very reluctant to remain silent on the topic. Still, both the pain and the peace kept increasing.

I recognized that he needed more time to understand our faith and let go of me, and I needed more time to let go of controlling his reaction and his blessing on my life choices. After several weeks, I received an email from him in which he expressed his desire to be reconciled. I later found out that after several sleepless nights he went to the earliest Mass at a local parish and heard the words of Jesus addressed to Martha, "You are anxious and troubled about many things; one thing is needful. Mary has chosen the good portion, which shall not be taken away from her." He knew in his heart then that Martha stood for married life, and Mary symbolized consecrated life—that even though his daughter would "miss out" on many things, she would be doing the one thing that is necessary, and it cannot be taken away.

This time in my life showed me that Jesus really does speak to us in our hearts and guides us to a deeper truth than we are conscious of. I also realized that God knows and works so intimately with us, that no other human being could do the same—I could have made convincing intellectual or moral arguments in my favor, but I could not have reassured him that consecrated life can be one filled with a personal love, fulfillment and meaning—something that any good friend hopes for someone he loves. This revelation was (and continues to be) transformative in my understanding of prayer as an authentic encounter with God that can change us and things around us.

—Reflection Questions—

1. Among the three aspects of prayer presented (real, intimate and transformative) where do I find some resistance in my heart? How can I bring this into conversational prayer with Jesus' presence?

2. What is one memory of a beautiful prayer that helps me remember the "taste" of authentic prayer?

GLORY

Mac Hill

*Already the glory of the risen Christ is reflected in
[Christians], transforming them to His image "of
glory unto glory" (2 Cor 3:18). By the Spirit even
suffering is transfigured (204).*

In this essay we will explore the Scriptural meaning of
glory and the share that we, as human beings, can have in it.
God is glory itself and He has revealed His glory to humanity,
especially through salvation history. Israel was glorified in being God's chosen people, but there was always a veil between
them and the full glory of God. The glory of God is revealed
more fully in the new covenant by the incarnation, passion,
resurrection, and subsequently by our transformation into the
image of Christ, who is glory incarnate. God reveals His glory
precisely in that He earnestly desires to share it with us, His
sinful, yet redeemed creatures. In fact, man's entire purpose is

that through the outpouring of the Holy Spirit "all of us, gazing with unveiled face on the glory of the Lord, are being transformed into the same image from glory to glory, as from the Lord who is Spirit" (2 Cor 3:18). A major theme of all Scripture is that God deeply desires to share His glory with us. This essay will thus build from the following: in man's relationship with God, glory has two major facets. He is earnestly calling us from glory to ever greater glory by sharing the likeness of Christ, and He is present in every moment, continually revealing His glory to us even in suffering.

First we must examine the meaning of the word "glory." The Hebrew word for glory is kabod, which involves the idea of weight. It is weight in the sense of the depth of something's existence and the respect it inspires/deserves. Glory in Hebrew is not so much renown as it is something's real value. The basis of glory could be riches—for example, Abraham was called very glorious because he owned cattle, silver, and gold (Gen 13:2). Glory could also signify high social status and authority, such as when Joseph says to his brothers, "Tell my father all the glory I have in Egypt" (Gen 45:13). The word also implies radiance and flashes of beauty, such as the glory of Aaron's vestments, the Temple, or Jerusalem. Above all, glory belongs to the king. Glory speaks of the luster and radiance of the king's reign, with his power and riches. For example, Solomon receives "riches and glory such as no other among the kings (1 Kgs 3:9-14)" (202-203).

Using this Scriptural understanding of glory, we understand more deeply what is meant by the fact that God, who is Being itself, desires to impart the depth of His Being with us and so created us to share in the inner life of the Trinity. In being glorified we are thus made weightier, more substantial beings; we are made whole. All of the other aspects of glory then follow; we are given splendor, heavenly riches, and authority because God has made us priests, prophets, and kings in Baptism.

Being brought from glory unto glory is centered on being formed into the likeness of Christ, who has been glorified by the Father. This glory has been won for us in Christ, and the Holy Spirit forms us into His likeness. The fullness of God in all His glory is entirely present in Christ; He is glory incarnate and the "splendor of His glory, the figure of His substance" (Heb 1:3). Paul tells us that the glory of God is "on His face" (2 Cor 4:6), meaning that when we see Christ we see the glory of God. Thus as we are ever more conformed to the likeness of Christ through the sacraments, prayer, good works, surrendering our will, participating in the passion and resurrection, etc., we are glorified. By God's grace this culminates in the beatific vision, which is to share fully in the inner life of the Trinity, beholding God in all His glory with an unveiled face in utter and complete union with Him. Again, considering the notion of glory as the weight of something's existence, by sharing in the glory of God, we become more full beings; we are made whole.

It is Jesus who shows us the way of glory unto glory. His glory was made manifest beginning with the Annunciation, when the "coming of the Holy Spirit upon Mary evokes the descent of the glory in the sanctuary" of the Temple (204). His glory is made manifest throughout His ministry, but the Father manifests it most fully in the Passion and Resurrection. Jesus consecrates Himself to the Father's will for the glory of His Name, and the Father in turn glorifies the Son in the Resurrection and Ascension. The water and blood that poured out from Jesus' side symbolize the fruitfulness of His death. Jesus abandoned Himself to the Father's will in full trust that the Father would glorify Him, as He prayed, "Now glorify me, Father, with you, with the glory that I had with you before the world began" (John 17:5). "Indifferent to glory among men" (John 5:41), He "despised the infamy of the cross" (Heb 12:2). His unique honor was to fulfill His mission, "not seeking His own glory," but "the glory of Him who sent Him" (John 7:18), putting His honor in the hands of His Father alone (John 8:50, 54) (205). Jesus' abandonment to the will of the Father is our roadmap to moving from glory to glory: we must abandon ourselves to trusting in the Father's providential will being at work in every little or big moment of our lives.

Connected to this journey to glory, is that the more intimately we share in the glory of God, the more we are able to see manifestations of His glory in our daily lives. Every time God manifests His presence to us it is a manifestation of His glory. He revealed His glory in the Old Testament in two ways: through His lofty deeds and through the apparitions of Himself. His mighty deeds, such as the wonder of creation, the liberation of Israel from Egypt, establishing a covenant with them, and conquering nations, revealed to Israel the glory of God. The appearances of God in the Old Testament showed forth His glory by the flashing radiance of the Divine Being. On Sinai, He covered the mountaintop with fire and smoke, and in the tent of meeting and the Temple He showed the wonder of His presence, yet there was always a veil between Israel and the glory of God. In the New Testament God revealed His glory in Jesus Christ and removed the veil between man and God's glory. St. Iraneaus tells us that Jesus Christ makes man the glory of God alive! God's glory is unveiled when we love and see our humanity alive in and through a relationship with Jesus. Therefore, if our eyes are open to the presence of God in our lives, we can see the glory of God every day.

A Personal Witness

God made His presence, and thus His glory, very apparent in my own life during my dad's battle with cancer. My dad had been sick with cancer for seven months when he suddenly took a turn for the worse. His health deteriorated so quickly that I basically had no other option but to abandon myself and my desire for my dad's healing to the Father's will. In this abandonment, He not only brought me from glory unto glory by conforming to Christ, but He also manifested His own glory in countless little ways during my dad's sickness. This culminated in the actual event of my dad's passing. While it was a painful experience, the glory of God shone on it in such a way that it was one of the most beautiful things I have ever seen. The details of the relating in love during this difficult time carry the "weight of God's glory." I can recall the event and its details with a luminous memory, clearly seeing the presence of God there. I have no doubt that my father is beholding the glory of the Father with an unveiled face right now, sharing in the glory of God.

Conclusion

In summary, God manifests His glory in manifold ways and He never ceases calling us to an ever greater glory in Him, which will culminate in the wedding feast of heaven. Jesus Christ is our example in that He freely received glory as a gift, in humility and trust. He did not take glory for Himself. His only concern was to fulfill His mission. Our calling is thus to abandon ourselves to the will of the Father, and His consoling graciousness, allowing Him to manifest Himself in us, and thus glorify us. This notion of glory adds new meaning to being a light in the world. By allowing God to manifest Himself in us, the radiance of Divine Being shines forth from us.

—Reflection Questions—

1. In what ways is the Father inviting me to surrender my will to Him so that I may be glorified in Jesus Christ?
2. In what ways has God manifested His glory in my life in the past? In what way(s) is He currently manifesting His glory in my life?

The Ascension of Christ, Gebhard Fugel, c. 1893

Sins and Sinfulness

Jeremy Lully

Before provoking man to act, sin corrupted his spirit; and affected him in his very relation to God of whom he is the image, a more radical perversion is inconceivable (550).

In our life of faith, sin is indubitably and inevitably present. We can never claim that we do not commit actions that offend God and our fellow brothers and sisters. When going to the sacrament of reconciliation, we make sure to examine our conscience and see what sins were committed by thought, word, deed, or omission. Sin will always be something that we struggle with, and knowing when we commit sin is certainly important, but understanding the root of these actions (our sinfulness) is more crucial, and can help us learn how to avoid sin and strengthen our relationship with God and others. The *Dictionary of Biblical Theology* provides a clear explanation on sinfulness, which sheds light on the troubling reality of sin.

Sin is the act that a person commits to reject the relationship of love God wants me to have with Him and with others. Also, sinfulness is the corruption of the spirit caused by confusing the understanding a person has of his relationship with God and with others. As a result, sin and sinfulness distance a person from God, which leads to his/her self-destruction.

In the Fall account of Genesis, sin first became present through disobedience but, what led to the act was a false understanding caused by sinfulness. Sinfulness caused man to believe that he had to compete against God, within a false belief that God would encroach upon man's freedom and desires. The consequences of sin manifested itself before the actual punishment. When Adam and Eve hid from God, this already was a sign of humanity's desire to have a different kind of relationship with Him; a relation that is not based on love. Banishment from the Garden of Eden was only a confirmation and result of mankind's decision to reject God and His love. This misunderstanding of God inevitably causes a misunderstanding of self and others. Adam's accusation of Eve shows how the person who was regarded as an equal, a helper (cf. Gen 2:18), is now put under his dominion (cf. Gen 3:16). Scripture makes clear how sin and sinfulness are damaging. Their proliferation throughout human history manifests itself through all social disorders such as violence, theft, false judgments, lies, adulteries, perjuries, homicides, usury, and disregard for rights (552).

All sin results in the same consequence of distancing a person from God, who is the source of his/her existence and being. This distancing without a doubt damages mankind, but it also offends God because Yahweh is not indifferent to man and the world. God is wounded by sin only because it hurts those whom He loves (552). To the extent that we contest against God's love and will for us, He cannot help but feel wounded because our sin is an act of ingratitude, and an act of infidelity to His faithfulness.

This reality is further revealed through Jesus Christ. The parable of the prodigal son shows how the Father's heart is saddened because the son no longer desires to be in a relationship of love with Him. The son, in a spirit of misunderstanding and disobedience, chooses to separate himself from the Father who loves him; thus, he took the riches of the Father before the proper time. The squandering of the riches and state of destitution that the son reaches are the self-destructive consequences of his sinfulness. His desire to return to the Father is his repentance, and this repentance is joyfully and readily accepted by the Father who Himself is mercy and forgiveness.

A Personal Witness

Reflecting on my youth, I am well aware of the many moments in which I have fallen into sin. One event is an incident that occurred between my grandma and me. When I was about thirteen years old, during summer afternoons I would usually go outside to hang out with a neighborhood friend. Normally whenever I was outside my grandma wanted me back inside around five o'clock. One day, I was having a good conversation with my friend and it was past five o'clock, I did not want to go inside, but my grandma told me that I could either come inside or I was going to get a whooping. To avoid embarrassment in front of my friend I went inside, but the moment I got inside the house I immediately made a dash to get back outside. Trying to stop me, my grandma grabbed the back of my shirt. I also grabbed the back of my shirt as I continued to run out. I thought I made a clean escape until I looked back and saw that my grandma had fallen. My pulling of the shirt had gone against hers and caused her to fall. Surprisingly, I did not get a whooping because my aunt came into the situation. When she found out what had happened, she said something to me (which at the time did not impact me as it does now). In the course of our conversation, my aunt referred to my grandmother as "mother." "She's not my mom; she's my grandma!" I said. My aunt quickly replied, "Yes, she is your grandma, but because she is your mother's mom, she is your mom also; so when you don't listen to her you don't listen to your mom." As I reflect upon those words, I can see how my sinfulness caused me to misunderstand my relationship with my grandmother and led me to disobedience. My grandma, out of her love for me (as her grandson), desired that I be safe. There were simple restrictions for when I could be outside in a violent neighborhood. When it began to become evening my grandmother wanted me inside the house. In my sinfulness, I misunderstood her as being the nagging old lady who did not want me to have fun. I failed to recognize that being responsible for my safety, she knew that at a certain time it was not safe to be outside. Rejecting her love for me, I also failed to realize that as my elder, and taking the place of my mother, I owed her loving obedience. This is why I committed that sin.

Sin is the act of rejecting the will of God, and His love (554). It is the obstacle *par excellence* to the glory of God; that which He desires to share with us (552). This rebelling against God comes from a spirit of sinfulness, the false understanding of the love of God. The apostles John and Paul understood sinfulness as that internal power or force of hostility toward God, and toward his reign. Sin, in turn, is only the exterior manifestation of that disposition of the heart (556). Sin draws us away from God and leads to our self-destruction. While this occurs to humanity, God does not stay idle. Sin would not be adequately understood without also knowing of the love and mercy of God. God, who becomes wounded by our sins, uses that obstacle *par excellence* as a tool to bring about His salvation. Through the wounds and sacrifice of Jesus Christ on the cross, humanity no longer competes against God and against itself. Jesus Christ ended the competition for self-destruction. Once and for all, we can be liberated from sinfulness and receive full remission for committed sins by living in relationship in everyday faith with Jesus Christ. As we repent of sin and the interior sinfulness of attitudes that draw us away from living in friendship with Jesus Christ, we receive an in-filling of mercy that heals and provides new peace and joy. Life is made new!

—Reflection Questions—

1. What is an internal temperament or attitude that provokes or motivates me to sin?
2. How have I recognized God's grace as healing mercy for my sinfulness?

CONVERSION AND REPENTANCE

Emmanuel Kyere Antwi

If Jesus has come, then he has come to call sinners to conversion (486).

Introduction

Conversion can be explained as God's call to men to enter into communion with Him (486). Reflecting on how Léon-Dufour treated this topic in his *Dictionary of Biblical Theology*, I was struck by his point that, "If Jesus has come, then he has come to call sinners to conversion" (486). This, according to Léon-Dufour, is an essential aspect of the gospel of the kingdom. I was specifically drawn to this sentence because of my personal experience and my interactions with other people. In this essay I will show that conversion is firstly God's initiative for humanity, and that each person is invited to respond to God's call to conversion positively in his own life.

Conversion and Repentance in the Old Testament

In the Old Testament, the terms conversion and repentance were employed to denote the re-establishment of the union between God and man. External acts of penance, such as fasting (see Judg 20:26), putting on sackcloth (see 1 Kgs 20:31f), rolling in ashes (see Isa 58:5), crying or groaning (see Judg 2:4), and sacrificing animals (see Lev 16:3), were used to express true repentance. The problem is that these acts usually became solely exterior gestures without the people engaging in them with their whole hearts. This, in effect, did not amount to genuine repentance.

Christ's Call to Conversion and Repentance

What does it mean when we say that Christ has come to call sinners to conversion? First, we must understand what sin is and why God has taken the initiative. A sinner is a person who commits an offence against reason, truth, and right conscience. Sin, in itself, is a failure in genuine love for God and neighbor, caused by a perverse attachment to certain goods.

Human beings are beset with so many weaknesses. These weaknesses sometimes lead us to find ourselves in either one sin or the other. Since sin is the only thing that can destroy our union with God, He willingly takes the initiative to call all sinners back to Himself. This is the reason why it is important that we pay particular attention to Christ's call to conversion.

God's Initiative and Humanity's Response to the Call to Conversion

One thing that we cannot lose sight of is the fact that the call to conversion comes about as a result of God's immeasurable love for humanity. It is God who takes the initiative to call man to conversion. This can be clearly demonstrated in the parable of the lost sheep (see Luke 15:4ff). It is the Good Shepherd who makes the decision to leave the ninety-nine sheep behind to go in search of the one sheep that is lost. When someone gets lost as a result of sin, God defies all odds to go in search of that person. In other words, it is the grace of God that calls man to conversion.

Having stated that the initiative to conversion comes from God, we must acknowledge the human response to Christ's call to conversion. When somebody ordinarily calls another by name, the one who is being called can choose either to respond to that call in an affirmative way or otherwise. The same scenario can be applied to God's call to conversion: God calls out to us, and we are left with the decision to accept His invitation or not.

Christ's call to conversion is both a general appeal to the entire human race and to each individual. As the Good Shepherd, Christ would not like any of His sheep to remain lost.

That is why He has made this general appeal, calling everybody to conversion. As free human beings, however, we can either decide to respond positively or negatively to this call to conversion. By responding positively to God's call, we should be prepared to turn away from our sinful deeds and allow the Spirit of God to direct all our actions, thoughts, and deeds. Ultimately, we are saying "yes" to the encounter with His mercy and love that transforms our lives.

In the parable of the prodigal son, we are told that the son, after wasting his life, decided to go back to his father. The son could have decided to die in his poverty. But he decided to go back to his father, who was already anticipating him with open arms. In our own lives, the Father is already expecting us with open arms and running toward us with merciful love. The decision whether to respond to His call positively or negatively, however, depends on us.

St. John Chrysostom's Steps to Conversion and Repentance

I would like to present some steps that can be followed so as to embrace genuine repentance. These five steps have been outlined by St. John Chrysostom. A first path of repentance, according to St. John Chrysostom, is the condemnation of our own sins. He writes, "Be the first to admit your sins and you will be justified."[1] The second point is to put out of our minds the harm done us by our enemies in order to master our anger and to forgive our fellow brothers' sins against us. Then, our own sins against the Lord will be forgiven us. The third step consists of prayer that is fervent and careful and which comes from the heart. The fourth step is almsgiving. Finally, the fifth step that St John Chrysostom addresses is humility: "If, moreover, a man lives a modest, humble life, that, no less than the other things I have mentioned, takes sin away. Proof of this is the tax-collector who had no good deeds to mention, but offered his humility instead and was relieved of a heavy burden of sins."[2] These general steps are meant to encourage and direct us to the practical reality of embracing God's grace of conversion for our lives.

A Personal Witness

I personally witnessed true repentance through an encounter that I had with a certain lady some time ago. This lady paid me a very surprised visit one morning. One could easily tell from her appearance that she looked very miserable. In fact, she had lost every hope in this world. This was a twenty-four-year-old girl who had already committed eight successive abortions. She was, as a matter of fact, very accustomed to fornication. As a way of sustaining herself in such a habit, she had resorted to the abuse of drugs of various kinds. After she had told me her story, she felt so worthless and miserable. With tears flowing down her cheeks, she asked if there was any hope for her.

In my confusion, I did not know what to say. After pausing for a while, I could hear myself telling her in a very soft voice: "Yes…there is still hope for any sinner who repents." I then advised her to see a priest, so as to avail herself to the sacrament of reconciliation. The point that I am trying to make is that hope is closely linked to conversion. Christ's call to conversion is supposed to give us the assurance that we can always be reconciled with God, no matter how serious our sins may be. She received hope and I could see that her tears spoke of the desire within her heart that longed to be received with merciful love. The gift of faith helped me to see the Holy Spirit at work in her tears and her question.

Conclusion

It can be deduced from all that has been said that only repentance prepares man to face the judgment seat. In order that we might not be found wanting on that day, we are being called by Christ to genuine conversion and repentance. As stated in the essay above, God, in the abundance of His mercy, does not want to lose any of us. That is why He makes a general and a particular call to conversion. He calls out to all humanity to turn to Him and asks each of us personally to affirm that call and embrace true repentance in our lives. The decision as to whether we are going to respond positively to this call or not remains our free choice. This being said it is especially important in the call to conversion to notice the initiative of God. In faith we recognize the desire, the longing itself within our hearts to be known in our original human dignity, as the Holy Spirit at work, loving us first.

—Reflection Questions—

1. Am I genuinely living in faith within the goodness of everyday repentance, responding to Jesus Christ's love calling me to conversion?
2. As a Christian, how do I lead others into recognizing the initiative of the Holy Spirit at work in our desires, inviting us into the goodness of conversion and repentance?

SALVATION

Logan Urban

To be saved is to be taken out of a dangerous situation in which one risks perishing. According to the nature of the danger, the act of saving manifests itself in protection, liberation, ransom, cure, victory, and peace (519).

Being saved is a concept to which all people can relate. Certainly, there are moments in everyone's life when we are desperate for God. As Christians, we should have more faith that God will come to our rescue. When we read the Bible, we should put ourselves in the shoes of the tax collectors and sinners. Jesus meets us where we are; whether it is in a gutter or a sports car. He calls all sinners (all of us) to repentance, which then leads to knowing and tasting the goodness of God's salvation.

Jesus scandalized the Pharisees by eating with tax collectors and sinners. Jesus affirms, "I have not come to call the righteous, but sinners to repentance" (Luke 5:32).[1] He went further by proclaiming to the Pharisees, "since sin is universal, those who pretend not to need salvation are blind to themselves" (cf. John 8:33-36).

In today's culture, people carry excess baggage. I'm speaking in general terms. It is not an outrageous assertion to suggest that people have skeletons in their closets more than ever, and those skeletons can creep up on us sometimes. Life, in a sense, is a battle, and the reason for this conflict is love! It is more than OK to call out to God if you need help. He will always hear you, and will always help you, even though it may not be in the way you expect. Once you figure out who you are—a child of God—you will be more inclined to follow His path and live in the beauty of knowing love in everyday life. And that, my friends, leads to understanding in all sorts of practical ways, salvation!

A Personal Witness

I experienced a form of salvation this summer at World Youth Day in Krakow, Poland. During this trip, there were times when our group had to walk many miles among millions of people. I remember when we were outside for forty-eight hours. A bus was scheduled to come pick us up at a designated location. Because millions of people were leaving the town on

---

1   Also consider Luke 18:9f, and John 9:34.

foot, the bus had trouble getting into the city. We were outside in the pouring rain for four hours waiting for this bus to save us! Many of the people in my group were suffering from ordinary weariness and some injuries from having walked a great deal. A sense of mild fear could be sensed as tough conditions were endured. Some of the kids started shivering intensely, all due to the weather conditions.

Being in a different country and not being able to read any of the street signs was not a pleasant experience. We were utterly desperate to be saved, so-to-speak. And, I will admit I had lost faith in the bus being able to arrive and find us. Some irrational fears began to be experienced, and on looking back I needed to trust more in the saving love of God at work in all circumstances. I will never forget the moment when the bus pulled up next to our group and opened the doors. Everyone screamed with relief. The mothers and daughters were all crying with tears of joy. When I got on the bus, I felt the warmth, and the softness of the seats. I recall falling asleep the moment I sat down. I had been so weary.

Humanity in a real sense is a damsel in distress, and God is our knight in shining armor. If you ever find yourself having car trouble or stranded on the side of the road or even just lost and surrounded by darkness and different forms of fear (small or great), remember that you will be saved by love in the situation in which you seem to be perishing. You will experience (in some way) being a passenger on the "bus" of God, where you will find protection, peace, liberation, ransom, and personal care. He is victorious over fear and weariness. His "bus" always comes to transport us into comfort in the midst of sufferings, assuring us by His loving presence with us.

—Reflection Questions—

1. What is holding me back from fully depending on God to save me by love in the events of everyday life?
2. How can I cultivate gratitude for the times when I have experienced God's love saving me from harm?

LOVE

Alexander J. Sanchez Rivera

*Man should purify the completely human concepts
he has made for himself about love, in order to
grasp the mystery of divine love—and this takes
place through the cross (322).*

From the very beginning of creation we can see that God created all things to be at our will and pleasure. He created a world for Himself and all of humanity to be able to live in a mutual love for one another. Our very creation is a sign of God's immense love for all of humanity, and the way we choose to live out our creation is the response of our love for Him. Love, as we see in the Scriptures, is a free and pure emptying of oneself to the other, that they may experience freedom and purpose in life. How is this love then acted out, so we can be in union with God the Father? Jesus, as our primary example, shows us that it is an obedience and fidelity lived out daily that manifests itself as love.

From the moment of creation God enters into "a dialogue of love with men; in the name of this love He binds them and teaches them to love each other" (322). We can see this through the relationship between Adam and Eve. As Fr. Léon-Dufour mentions, "God wishes to give them life in its fullness, but this gift supposes free adherence to His will" (322). This love is so intense that even when Adam and Eve break away from that bond by going against His commandment, this same break is seen revealing God's mystery of goodness, as the break opens up the infinite well of mercy. God does not finish the conversation when we break away from Him; instead, He continues to invite us deeper into dialogue with Him (323). Even though there was a rupture between God and man at that moment it was not the end. God then waits for those whom He finds ready and willing to receive Him. God expresses love to His chosen people through leaders whom He sends: Abraham, Moses, David, etc.

This dialogue of love is then brought to fulfillment with the coming of Jesus, *the Word made flesh*. The words preached by the prophets, kings and patriarchs now dwell with man. "Jesus came to enter deeply into the dialogue of love in a personal manner" (324). Fr. Léon-Dufour beautifully states: "Jesus is God come to live out His love in the fullness of humanity and who came to make us understand the ardent appeal of love. In His very person man loves God and is loved by Him" (324). How does Jesus do this? He does what Adam and Eve would not: He is obedient to the will of His Father. It is in the acceptance of His brutal passion that the dialogue is brought to fulfillment. This serves as the quintessential example of how the Christian continues the dialogue of love. Jesus enters ahead of us into our passions, our sufferings. Whenever we relate to Him from where we are most broken, most distant from knowing that His love is with us, we are surprised to find Him waiting for us. Jesus is present in our brokenness ready to console us and carry us into the joy of the Father's presence as merciful love.

A Personal Witness

This past summer I participated in a summer program of intense spiritual formation for Catholic seminarians. Part of the program is an eight-day Ignatian retreat. One of the texts we encountered at the beginning of the summer, a text which stayed with me and invited me into deep prayer, reads:

Nothing is more practical than
finding God, than
falling in Love
in a quite absolute, final way.
What you are in love with,
what seizes your imagination, will affect everything.
It will decide
what will get you out of bed in the morning,

LOVE

what you do with your evenings,
how you spend your weekends,
what you read, whom you know,
what breaks your heart,
and what amazes you with joy and gratitude.
Fall in Love, stay in love,
and it will decide everything.[1]

These inspiring words would revolutionize my time in the summer program. The grace I was led to ask for during my retreat was, "to grow in greater freedom and intimacy with God the Father." He was the one person in the Trinity from whom I had felt distant. As the retreat began, I immediately started seeing and experiencing God's love for me. At the mid-point of the retreat I was brought back to a lot of painful moments in my life where I had felt far from the Father's love and acceptance. Once I was able to overcome these and be utterly honest, allowing myself to be naked in front of the Father. He took me to the places where I was distant from Him and did not feel a mutual love. I could feel the Lord inviting me into those places to love Him deeply and to allow myself to be loved deeply. What He asked of me was to grow in greater obedience and fidelity to Him, as He asked of Adam and Eve years ago. He asked me to

---

1 Attributed to Fr. Pedro Arrupe, S.J. See: Wild, Robert Anthony and Stephanie Russell, ed., *Finding God in All Things: A Marquette Prayer Book,* Milwaukee: Marquette University Press, 2005.

be vigilant in tough times, as Jesus was in the garden. He asked me to no longer look back and always be disposed to His will in my life. I cannot say that I have done this perfectly since then, but for the times that I have, I have experienced God's love in a liberating manner. I discovered and continue to discover that the Father's love is eager to be poured into our hearts at those points of greatest hurt or shame.

Conclusion

When we look back at the references in the Scriptures to God's dialogue of love, we can note interestingly enough, that some of these major points of dialogue happen in two gardens: the Garden of Eden (Gen 3) and the Garden of Gethsemane (Matt 26:36-46). In the Garden of Eden, Adam and Eve, who were in a perfect dialogue with God's love, broke away from it by not following God's command at work protecting them. In the Garden of Gethsemane Jesus accepts the Father's will for Him regardless of how much suffering-love it causes Him. The cross is the perfect example, not only of God's love for us, but for how we are called to return love to God. Falling in love with God is utterly wonderful, a saving grace, but to be able to stay in love with God calls for daily decisions that respond to His dialogue of love. We remain in His love when we surrender to permitting Him to love us where we have experienced hurts and often hide from ourselves and from God. Remaining in love with Jesus also calls us in faith to reject all of those inner attitudes that carry us into the pain of believing something other than the truth that we are the Father's beloved sons and daughters. We are called to exercise faith in daily decisions to remain in love. This gives us a taste of the reign of God. In a real sense by remaining faithful to living in a dialogue of love we can experience Jesus' desires to walk freely in the "garden" of our hearts with mercy, love and delight!

—Reflection Questions—

1. In what ways have I experienced the dialogue of love that God is always offering?
2. Am I willing to ask for new faith to permit the risen Jesus to walk freely in the "garden" of my heart? What would the hesitations be to further enter into this dialogue of love?

HOPE

Nathanael Soliven

Rooted in this way in faith and trust, hope can open out toward the future and sustain the whole life of the believer with its dynamism (240).

In Sacred Scripture, the word "hope" is very closely connected to some Hebrew, Greek and Latin roots[1] that have these common meanings if translated to English: to trust or to have confidence in, to anticipate, to persevere and endure, to support or to sustain, and to wait for salvation with joy and full confidence.[2] Thus we could see how even from the definitions alone, hope is inevitably tied to faith and love. As Fr. Léon-Dufour says, the theological virtues of faith, hope and love are "different aspects of one spiritual complex" (240).

---

1   Hebrew: *qāwāh, yāhal* and *bātah;* Greek: *elpizō, elpis, pepoitha, hypomenō;* Latin: *spero, spes, confido, sustineo, expecto.*

2   *Online Dictionaries,* accessed September 30, 2016, http://www.biblestudytools.com and http://latin-dictionary.net.

Anchored in the **resurrection** and the *Parousia* of our Lord, the Church's hope ignites and sustains the individual hope of all its members making them joyful and steadfast even in the midst of suffering, confident that glory awaits those who continue to have faith and love.

The *Parousia*

The hope of the entire church is strongly centered on the *Parousia*, the second coming of Christ. The glory of the *Parousia* is so abundant that it flows even in its mere anticipation in the present. This is the reason why a lot of the martyrs of the church have willingly and confidently died for their faith: Because even in the midst of persecution, they were already experiencing the glory of God. As Fr. Léon-Dufour mentions, "The Church's hope is joyful even in suffering" (241).

The Resurrection

For St. Paul, not believing in the resurrection is the same as being without hope. Through the resurrection, Christ leads men, whom Adam has dragged toward death, back to life. Because Christ rose from the dead and ascended body and soul to heaven, we know that there is life after death. We are confident that if we continue to have faith, hope and love, we will meet our creator someday face to face. We will finally be in perfect communion with the Trinity, the deepest desire of all our desires; that ultimate happiness that every human being seeks but desperately attempts to find in the lower goods of this world whether in grand vanities of power, richness and glory or in simple desires of relationships, food or whatever object to which we cling. We demand from these lower goods a full satisfaction of our desires and a completion of that emptiness in us, but they cannot because they are not God. But believing in the resurrection, we are filled with hope that someday, despite the seemingly unending trials of the present, we will be in the presence of our Beloved Creator. When that happens, our restless hearts will finally find rest in Him and we will desire nothing more.

A Personal Witness

In an apostolic assignment that I was serving in I met Jenny (*not her real name*) who for me was a woman of great hope. Jenny works for an institution where I used to volunteer weekly. She was a mother of three children and she was very warm, friendly, caring and dedicated to her work. There was an event in the seminary that Thursday which she agreed to attend to with her son, but they never showed up. The following Monday, I saw Jenny in her usual warm aura and smile and I asked her how she was because I didn't see them at the event. Her light countenance suddenly changed to a serious one but still calm. She then shared that her teenage daughter had been undergoing counseling because of drugs, skipping school and other problems. During that week's session, the counselor discovered that the daughter had been sexually abused by Jenny's boyfriend who was living with them in the same house. That happened on a Wednesday and the police came to their house on Thursday to interrogate Jenny's boyfriend. The next day, Friday, Jenny's boyfriend committed suicide. While she was telling me this, I was just amazed at how Jenny was sharing all of this in a calm manner despite the fact that this happened only four days ago. At the end of our short conversation, she mentioned that, amidst the anger and helplessness, she was comforted by the gospel, which spoke that day of the poor Lazarus being in heaven and the indifferent rich man in hell. She was hopeful that whatever happened she and her daughter would surpass this trial and move on. Jenny continued to work with us that same day and she remained calm. She was as normal as ever, happy and warm to all those with whom we interacted.

Conclusion

Reflecting on Jenny's sharing, I realized that her hope was not just some shallow optimism but a profound Christian hope. Her hope is actually anchored in the resurrection and the *Parousia,* which is manifested by her short allusion to the justice and recompense in the life after death as seen in the gospel. Jenny's hope opened her seemingly crumbling life toward a future in the Lord that continued to sustain her. That hope was what gave her peace and made her joyful and steadfast in her faith in the midst of her suffering. That hope continued to affect and strengthen God's gifts of faith and love inside of Jenny.

Like Jenny and like many great Christians, St. Paul also exhibited a valuable witness of hope, and it is with this that I would like to close. Fr. Léon-Dufour mentioned that after all of Paul's work in the missions, which was accompanied both by joy and sadness, when his death seemed near, he only hoped for one thing—to be with the Lord. In the end, Paul is "no longer looking forward to his personal happiness but quite simply to being with someone he loves" (242).

—Reflection Questions—

1. In what particular instances of my life did hope sustain me in the midst of difficulties?
2. How do I see and understand the interaction and inseparable activity of faith, hope and love in my life?

The Resurrection of Jesus Christ,
Jacopo Tintoretto, 1565

THE HOLY SPIRIT

John Armon S. Antolin

*He always acts through another person, when He takes pos-
session of him and transforms him... [and] His action always
proceeds from the interior and it is from the interior
that you recognize Him (571).*

Heart of the Matter

Who is the Holy Spirit? Before the widely influential char-
ismatic renewal, the Holy Spirit could be considered the forgot-
ten Person of the Trinity. The Father and the Son are often called
upon in prayer and are more noticeable in Scripture, and even
the images we typically use for the Holy Spirit are often difficult
to grasp: water, fire, oil, wind, breath, a dove, etc. At the same
time, while the Spirit can be ignored or misinterpreted, one cannot deny that the Spirit has been at work with the Father and the
Son for all eternity and within the Church throughout her entire

history. This mysterious force that invades us and saturates us with His presence shows Himself as the primary transformer of reality, a transformation that flows from deep within the person, where the Spirit has found His home.

The Spirit of Transformation

In the Old Testament, the Holy Spirit is present, but not fully revealed, for Christ—the Word Incarnate—has not yet acted in the Spirit or promised the Spirit's coming. Before creation, the *Spirit of God* is found hovering above the waters (Gen 1:2). This same *Spirit of God* is the *breath* that uttered the Word through which all things came to be in the beginning (John 1:1-3). The Spirit is also described as the *wind*, such as the one that divided the Red Sea (Exod 14:21). The Spirit is life-giving, as can be seen when He blew like *wind* over the sea of dry bones and revived those very bones by His *breath* (Ezek 37:9-10). This is the same Spirit that Christ was filled with in His very being. For Christ, the Spirit did not invade Him, but was in Him, as He was in the Spirit. The Holy Spirit is the creator and transformer of reality. Saints are able to find God in all things and all things in God because of the Spirit's transformative work.

This transformative work happens not only in external re-alities, but deep within the internal reality of every person. The Holy Spirit "always acts through another person," as shown by the patriarchs, judges, kings, and prophets of the Old Testament (571). The story of most of these figures can be outlined: first, the person is often regarded as insignificant, yet God calls him or her to a mission. Second, the person is reluctant because of their fears and doubts, but God blesses or anoints that person so that the *Spirit* descends and remains. Third, that person, given a new strength and confidence in his or her vocation, perseveres through struggles with and in the Spirit in order to carry out the mission to which God has called him or her.

One could say that this is the story of every disciple of Christ; the Spirit has been actively transforming the Church from Peter all the way down to us. This call of the Spirit is a call heard from within; it is the very *breath* that gives us life. In God's language of silence, this unique call is heard in one's heart. This call is so unique that the one being called is given the opportunity to transform reality, themselves and others. The action of the Spirit becomes the action of the disciple who listens and communes with Him; in other words, the disciple is transformed and is able to transform.

How Did I Do That?

One of the most uncomfortable pastoral ministry services for me is teaching children, because I do not see myself as a good teacher. I do not always know how to relate to children because I did not have any siblings growing up—I was also a timid child. On top of that, I am keenly aware of how delicate teaching a child is, because as I have seen in my past, the things my teachers taught me in catechism were very influential for me in both good and not-so-good ways. Nevertheless, in God's humor, I was asked to teach catechism to a middle school class during my summer at Holy Spirit Catholic Church in Jacksonville. The pastor also kindly asked me to join the children (from kindergarten to eighth grade) in their weekly summer camps.

As the summer started and I joined the children in their various camps, the beginning was very difficult. I was nervous because I did not know any of the children there or how to relate to them, and I was the first seminarian ever sent to that parish. Over time, however, the worries and fears slowly faded away. When I immersed myself in the ministry, it just felt like I was playing with the kids—I was a kid again, a seminarian kid. The week eventually came for me to teach and once again, fears, doubts, and hesitations rose within me. I remember buying the supplies I needed for class and preparing the lesson plans for the following day—which sometimes lasted until the morning hours. Yet again, when I immersed myself in the ministry, the fears and doubts faded away.

By the end of the summer, I became part of that parish and school community. The people knew me and I knew them. We all encouraged and challenged each other in our actions and in our words. Sometimes, the hardest thing to admit is that the Holy Spirit can transform me to be holy, to be a saint; but in a profound way, the Holy Spirit showed me that I can relate and minister to children. I asked myself: "How did I do that?" At those moments when all the fears and doubts dissipated and I was immersed in the service and self-giving, transformation occurred: it was no longer I who lived, but the Spirit within me.

Who is the Holy Spirit?

Again we ask: "Who is the Holy Spirit?" The Holy Spirit is the transformer of reality and of people. This mysterious Person is not only the transformer, but the transformation. In this transformation, His presence is made evident in creation and in our daily lives. The transformation of the Spirit occurs deep within us, but it is from this point that His power overflows like a font which transforms not only ourselves, but others.

—Reflection Questions—

1. Can I recount and describe a personal experience when the Holy Spirit transformed me or others around me?
2. Is there a Biblical image of the Holy Spirit that particularly speaks to my experience of the Spirit's active presence in daily life?

The Annunciation, Henry Ossawa Tanner, 1898

FATHERS & FATHER

Leo Siqueira

But when the fullness of time had come, God sent his Son ...
so that we might receive adoption. As proof that you are chil-
dren, God sent the spirit of his Son into our hearts, crying out,
"Abba, Father!" (Gal 4:4-5).

In the fullness of time, the Father sent His Word, His essence to be made flesh to dwell among us. God sent his on-
ly-begotten Son, "wanting to make us sharers in his divinity,
assumed our nature, so that he, made man, might make men
gods."[1] Our destiny is to be with the Father for eternity. In this
mystery, the absolute apex of God's love is revealed: He does
not only call us His children, but He goes beyond that, calling
us to be His children in the complete sense of the word. He asks
us to partake in His divinity by being His sons and daughters.

It is only through this relationship between the Father and

---

1   St. Thomas Aquinas, Opusc. 57, 1-4. (CCC 460)

the Son that we can be a son of God. Likewise, it also is in this relationship between the Father and Son that the earthly fatherhood finds its perfection. Hence, by diving into the mystery of the supreme relationship between the fatherhood of God and the sonship of Jesus, mankind will be restored to his true identity, namely, being the sons and daughters of God having been made in His image and likeness.

Jesus Reveals the Father

In the seventeenth chapter of John, we find one of the most beautiful dialogues between Jesus and His Father. In this conversation, we see the very mission and the reason why Jesus was killed: "Give glory to your son, so that your son may glorify you… Now this is eternal life, that they should know you, the only true God, and the one whom you sent, Jesus Christ. I glorified you on earth by accomplishing the work that you gave me to do" (John 17:1-4). What is the work that the Father gave to His only Son? This work or mission is to bring salvation to all men by sharing through the Incarnation the very being of God for eternity. This salvation came only because Jesus revealed His true identity as the Son of God.

There can be no father without a son and there could be no son without a father. For this very reason, sonship is at the heart of fatherhood. In Jesus, there is a perfect notion of filiation that brings the paternity of God to man. When God made himself visible through Incarnation, He used our own language to communicate with us. In Jesus' human nature He needed to experience earthly things (except sin) in order to redeem us. In the same way, the relationship of Jesus with His heavenly Father in the Incarnation begins here on earth.

All human experiences, without exception, begin at the natural level. God chose Joseph to be the earthly father of Jesus. In this relationship we see the transcendence of the Father's paternity realized in the person of Joseph. This transition from Joseph's fatherhood to the Heavenly Fatherhood can be seen in the relation between the Old and New Testament: "Between the human fathers and God a likeness exists which permits the name of father to be applied to the latter" (171).

Jesus Reflects the Father

"Let us make human beings in our image, after our like-ness" (Gen 1:26). Most of the Fathers of the Church distin-guished between the image and likeness. The image is the sum of the possibilities for the realization of the likeness, namely, the potentialities of the likeness of God. The likeness, on the other hand, is formed by the fulfillment of the image. The image is natural while the likeness is virtual (by virtues). Respectively, one is possessed by creation and the other is acquired by the will.[2] The reason the Church Fathers made this distinction was

---

2   Jean-Claude Larchet, *Therapy of Spiritual Illness*, vol. 1, 17.

to connect the virtues with likeness.

This distinction is important in order to understand the Father's plan of salvation in the person of His son, Jesus. The intimacy with the Father is acquired through virtues, meaning, through prayer on which the will is needed. This can clearly be seen in the life of Jesus. When Jesus taught us how to pray, He said, "Our Father." For this reason, Fr. Léon-Dufour says the sonship of Christ is at the heart of prayer. When I desire or say that I want to be like this or that person, I do not mean physically, but in virtues. I envision the qualities of that person, namely, his or her virtues.

Jesus' mission to make the Father known to all of us is to give us awareness of His very presence in our midst. Consequently, it leads us to a life that is similar to God's life, his likeness.[3] "Whoever has seen me has seen the Father" (John 14:9). God primarily communicates His likeness to us on a created level, which means that the person is made in the image of God, then, secondly, in His likeness, which is to be acquired.

God, through the self-giving of His only Son, communicated to us His very being, which is love. In other words, man becomes like God when his life is lived in the way of love. Jesus' filial love is manifested through the Spirit because the Spirit is the interior agent of Jesus' adoption, which became a universal adoption. On the other hand, our filial love is expressed through

---

3   Marko Ivan Rupnik, *Discernment Acquiring the Heart of God*, (Boston: Pauline Books & Media, 2006), 12.

prayer and fraternal charity. By loving the Father, we should love His children, the ones who were given to Jesus by the Father: "Holy Father, keep them in your name that you have given me, so that they may be one just as we are" (John 17:11). The virtues lead us to love one another. By doing that we are imitating the Trinity, where this mutual love is lived perfectly.

A Personal Witness

The earliest memory I have of my father was when I was five or six years old. I consider that memory as one of the most wonderful graces I have received. The image is still clear in my mind until this very day. In the village in Brazil where I grew up, it was very common for people to sit on the sidewalks and spend time chatting and relaxing. I remember my father wearing his pajamas sitting in front of Zaza's Shoe Repair one weekend. I had just finished playing with my brother and friends and I was standing close to him. He suddenly grabbed me, put me on his lap, embraced me and kissed me. That image comes to my prayer very often and it gives me a tremendous sense of peace and security. The image that comes to my mind when this memory arises is that of Hosea 11:4, "I fostered them like those who raise an infant to their cheeks." Like the Heavenly Father, my earthly father took care of his child and, when the right time came, he sent his child to a mission to be a man of virtue and to mature spiritually as the image of Jesus that I am.

In this living memory is a fountain of grace. I receive often from the Spirit, blessing me with love, as my earthly father's actions mediated my Heavenly Father's desires to kiss and embrace me always. The practice of virtue is made more attractive and fulfilling whenever I surrender my will to receiving my Heavenly Father's affections in the Spirit. Believing myself to be one within Jesus as Son, I am motivated by love to become more like Him in the practice of Christian virtues and in living charitably for others.

Conclusion

After reading Fr. Léon-Dufour's discussion on "Fathers & Father," what caught my attention was this deep relationship between the Father and Son that led me to find my own identity. When I call my parents, the first thing they say when they pick up the phone is, "Hi, my son. God bless you." These words give me a sense of belonging every time I hear it. They call me by my very identity: son. I realized that there is nothing better than knowing that I belong to someone. This brings me peace and stability.

In order to fulfill our destiny, which is to live with and in the Father for eternity, we have to live in a sense of belonging as His sons and daughters. The sonship of Jesus restores this brotherhood once lost by sin. Through Jesus the Father reconciled mankind back to Himself. In the very name of Jesus, we can see the purpose of His mission. Jesus means "God saves" and Christ means "messiah" (anointed). Jesus is the one who reveals and reflects the Father's image and likeness in its full-ness to mankind. In the Son, the earthly fatherhood finds its perfection. Only in the Son and through the activity of the Holy Spirit can we become perfect like our heavenly Father. This God-like form was only possible because in the fullness of time, the Father sent His Word, His essence to be made flesh to dwell among us.

—Reflection Questions—

1. What is the earliest memory that I have of my earthly father (or someone who represents him), and how can this memory lead to further reconciling, forgiving love of my heavenly Father?

2. How have I experienced being invited into knowing my heavenly Father's affection for me?

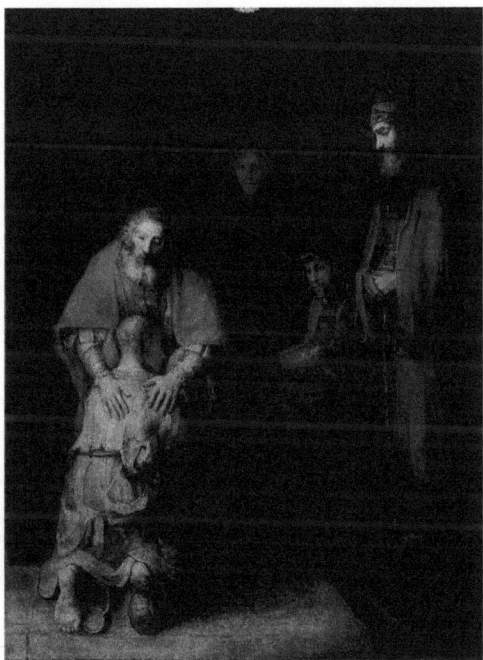

The Return of the Prodigal Son,
Rembrandt van Rijn, c. 1661–1669

THE CHURCH

Piotr Sawicki

The Church, the true people of Abraham, should insert itself in the world and there be the answer to sin, to its discords, and the death proceeding from sin (73).

This quote from the *Dictionary of Biblical Theology* closely resembles the understanding of the Church as the Sacrament of Salvation, articulated by the Second Vatican Council (cf. *Lumen Gentium*, §48), and promoted by the succeeding Popes. We are also reminded of the recent comparison made by Pope Francis: that the Church should act as a field hospital after battle, healing the wounds of the seriously injured.[1] It is not the righteous who need this aid, but sinners (cf. Mark 2:17). As the members of the Church who are privileged to receive much from her, we must in turn freely share with others the healing and the salvation that we

---

1　　Spadaro, Antonio, Interview with Pope Francis *"A Big Heart Open to God,"* (America magazine, Vol. 209 No. 8. Sept. 30, 2013).

experience in her, through the One to whom we are united.

Christ taught us that we should prefer service to looking for the places of honor, and in that service we should pay special care to the weak and lost (74). When we have this zeal and love for souls, we truly build up the Church, following the example of the Apostles and Saints (78). St. Paul in his letters compares the Church to the body of Christ, made of various members bestowed with different charisms for the good of all: *Now Christ's body is yourselves, each of you with a part to play in the whole* (1 Cor 12:27). Upon following the references provided by the Dictionary, we can see that St. Paul embedded the "Hymn to Love" (1 Cor 12:31-13:13) between exhortations to earnestly desire higher spiritual gifts. Perhaps St. Paul chose this placement of the "Hymn to Love" because the use of these gifts is the mission of her individual members, and can only be appropriately exercised when they are done out of love. Similarly, in the first letter of St. Peter we see that the gifts of the individuals should be exercised in love for the good of others (1 Pet 4:8-11). Whenever our service in the Church is not driven by this self-donating love (but by other motives such as a desire to feel good about oneself or to gain respect of others), we easily become like tasteless salt (cf. Matt 5:13). Our ministry may still seem fruitful on the surface through activities that help the poor, committing more time to parish life, etc. However, we would be effectively saying to the Lord: *Did we not prophesy, drive out demons and*

do mighty deeds in your name? If so, we will easily find ourselves faced with the answer *"I never knew you. Depart from
me, you evildoers"* (cf. Matt 7:21-23).

But it is not by our efforts that our actions are filled with
this divine flavor. It is our participation in the life of the Church
that enables us to live out the mission entrusted to her. It is in
her that Christ communicates His nature to us (75). We see it in
another image appearing in Pauline letters, where the Church is
seen as the bride of Christ. With the help of prophetic writings
we see how God restores our dignity in the Church and how He
enables us to live a life that is worthy of Him (73). We might
be familiar with the typological interpretation that sees Christ's
piercing (John 19:34) as a pentecostal outpouring of the Holy
Spirit making all things new, establishing a new creation. Jesus
as the new Adam is here revealed as Spouse. But, I believe we
can go a step further from those passages as we draw another
analogy between the Church's life and the life of her members
nourished by the sacraments (75). Reborn in Baptism, strengthened in Confirmation and nourished in the Eucharist, we become incorporated into Christ, who can then act in us for the
Glory of God. In order to retain the divine flavor of charity that
is at work in all things we need to remember that apart from
Him, we can do nothing (cf. John 15:5).

A Personal Witness

In this context, I would like to recall my experience with two homeless people I met some months before entering the seminary. Not to boast of myself, since if I did any good that evening, it certainly did not come from any of my qualities. I was just happy that God could work through me. The evening was late and cold and one of the homeless men had a friend who was just taken by an ambulance to the hospital. He was suffering because of overdosing on some kind of drug. In this seemingly hopeless situation I felt urged to accompany the homeless friends of this man, and share with them whatever I was able to, while not being too pushy. We bought some sandwiches and beer and sat in front of the Basilica of St. Mary in Gdańsk in Poland. I did not dare to explicitly announce with words the love that God had for them. I just hoped that Jesus' Spirit would enter this evening and transmit to them whatever they needed in that moment when they felt hopelessness. During our conversation, one of them spoke about having been tricked by another homeless man earlier that day, and in his anger he did not want to have anything to do with him. I thought about inviting him to forgive his friend for tricking him out of this small amount of money. But, after a brief reflection it seemed better to let the Holy Spirit speak directly to his heart through the events of this evening and my quiet presence. I hope that through the time we spent together I was able to mediate the Holy Spirit's loving presence and provide some opportunities for the Holy Spirit to work on their hearts. I felt that the Church, present in a particular way in the Basilica right in front of us, extended its walls to accompany us in friendship and offer hope. It was a blessing for me to see this in faith, and this memory gives me the desire to serve in this manner. Christ is so present in the poor, the homeless.

Conclusion

The *Dictionary of Biblical Theology* speaks of the Church as of a "life principle visible everywhere, a spiritual suggestion of an invisible, eternal kingdom where death will be destroyed" (74). As long as this principle remains within the walls of the temples, only for those who are already gathered there, its radiance is obscured. In one of the initial catechesis of the Neocatechumenal Way it is described as a false attempt at preservation, which in itself is insufficient for a parish to function properly. The Second Vatican Council reminds us that the Church is by her nature, missionary (cf. *Ad Gentes*, §2), while Pope Francis again and again calls us to go out of the walls of the churches in order to make Christ present where the people are—so that through Him, they may be brought back to the Father. Whenever the faithful, the living blocks of the Church, are enabled by the Sacraments to fulfill this mission entrusted to her, she truly becomes a light to the nations, so that God's salvation may reach the ends of the earth (cf. Isa 49:6).

—Reflection Questions—

1. When have I experienced the beauty of the Church in her poor?

2. Recently, how have I seen the Holy Spirit at work in my local Church?

REVELATION

Saul Araujo

God reveals His plans which trace the way of salvation for
men. He reveals Himself so that man may be
able to meet Him (500).

St. Irenaeus affirms: God's "revelation is salvation." He reveals his Law to us, how to turn back to him, how to be happy. This revelation is not something trivial. God reveals what enables man to fulfill himself as a being. He reveals himself in Scripture as one who cares for His creation, who makes and fulfills promises (as with Abraham), and who is always present to His people (as in the cloud and pillar of fire that led the Israelites in the desert). The Bible even mentions that Moses would speak to God face to face as with a friend (c.f. Exod 33:11). This implies that the biblical understanding of God is one which comes out of personal experience. He is a God who is known through His faithfulness in love and through personal encounter, not by mere philosophical and theological specu-lation. This is extremely relevant for us since God desires to reveal Himself to each of us in a personal way. Indeed, the full-ness of revelation only came when God stood before us person to person, when "the Word became flesh and made his dwelling among us" (John 1:14). In Christ, God has revealed Himself to us personally and perfectly, and this revelation is our salva-tion. The revelation of God began in the Old Testament, but it reached its fullness in the New Testament. As I once heard it said, "Christ is a tree which flourishes in the New Testament but with its roots in the Old Testament."

In short, God revealed Himself gradually through the Old Testament as He encountered and personally accompanied His chosen people. He revealed himself as the God who loves them and is able to save them from sin and oppression. This revela-tion reaches its culmination and perfection in the person of Jesus Christ, who alone can give us total victory over sin and death.

The Revelation of God in the Bible

Judaism, and consequently Christianity, are religions based on a reliable revelation, a revelation of love. We do not rely on the teachings and witness of a single founder or thinker, but on a mysterious God (in the positive sense of mystery) who has journeyed with His people through time. He is the transcen-dent God who chose to reveal Himself gradually through history, specially beginning with Abraham and notably to Moses and the Israelites who were but slaves. These partial and fragmentary forms of revelation are part of the same continuum of revelation that culminates in Jesus Christ, since it is the same God who has been accompanying His people from the beginning and who sends the Holy Spirit to overshadow and become Incarnate through the Virgin Mary.

How did God first reveal Himself? He initially appealed to the "natural religiosity" of the chosen people. Natural religiosity is the natural openness that we all possess toward that which is transcendent. From ancient times the human person discovered that he could not control many things around himself, such as natural disasters, illnesses, and death. He would attribute to gods or divine beings these extraordinary forces and events. We find in the Torah that this yearning for answers and explanations had taken shape and become divination, magic rituals, astrology, etc. As Fr. Léon-Dufour explains, God will use all of this to make Himself known to the Israelites. He will appear to Moses as a burning bush and use a language that Moses is familiar with as He imparts to him the promise of salvation for his people. This apparition, which would certainly be extraordinary for us today, was however fairly comprehensible to Moses because of the religiosity in his day.

Long after this specific event of the burning bush we see a crescendo in Scripture of how God will reveal Himself more and more, all for our salvation and fulfillment. He reveals

Himself through the *prophets* in visions and words that largely call for repentance and promise future salvation, and in *wisdom* which appeals to the intellect and invites them to live righteously according to the truth. He also reveals Himself *apocalyptically*, most especially seen in the book of Daniel, to remind His people of the cosmic scope of His revelation. By the time of the New Testament, God has already purified many of the Israelite religious customs, spirituality, and so forth, a process that began distinctly with His giving them the Decalogue (The Ten Commandments). The Israelites were the privileged people to whom God revealed His will. These revelations were unique gifts, gifts which speak of God's love and care because they are given to a fallen humanity precisely for the sake of salvation.

In the New Testament, we have come to know that God reveals Himself in fullness through His Son. Jesus says to Philip, "Whoever has seen me has seen the Father" (John 14:9). The last aspect of revelation in the Scriptures regards the book of Revelation. The concern here is no longer "the earthly life of Jesus, but is oriented toward His final manifestation to which the history of the Church and of the entire world is a prelude" (504). In this sense the Book of Revelation is a Christian prophecy of victory and liberation where the lamb shall destroy the beast, and those who are saved shall dwell forever in the heavenly Jerusalem.

A Personal Witness

In Jesus Christ we discover God's love in a personal way, and this is the *kerygma* (good news) of Christianity. God became Incarnate, took on our humanity and took our place in self-emptying death, and rose from the dead. I have seen the love of God and the power of His death and resurrection by witnessing the extraordinary love lived out between some of the people around me. I recall the case of a couple very close to me who overcame the sin of infidelity at a very early stage of their marriage through the power of forgiveness. I came to know the case through the wife and am an eyewitness of their forgiveness. I witnessed as well, the fruits which this forgiveness produced in their lives. To this day, these good fruits of peace and joy and gentleness affect not only themselves as spouses, but it includes their children and grandchildren. I can be sure that God loves, and that Christ has overcome death, when this type of forgiving love is made visible between His creatures. It is a divine, real love. The couple was able to forgive and love each other as Jesus Christ did, even when the other became as an "enemy." In this incident I witnessed the risen Christ granting them power over sin. Truly, God has revealed Himself in Jesus Christ so that we can be saved from our sins and learn to love as He loves. If we humans, limited and wounded by sin, can imitate God to this extent of forgiving love, we can only imagine how much greater is God's love for us, since He is love (see 1 John 4:8).

Conclusion

As humans, we yearn for the truth. There is in each one of us a kind of natural religiosity that looks out for an explanation, for meaning and direction. This leads us to recognize our need for experiencing the resurrected Christ present and acting in each of our daily lives. In Jesus Christ, God has revealed His plan of forgiving love for us and the world. He has revealed the truth of who He is and has "set us free" from sin and death (see John 8:32). Only a transcendent God who is "the same, yesterday, today, and forever" (Heb 13:8) can enlighten our history entirely and accompany us from its beginning to end. As we study and pray with the Scriptures we witness God as a reality, revealed and present in the life of the Israelites, God's chosen people. In Jesus Christ we see and experience the power of resurrected forgiving love. May we yearn all the more to live life in, through and with Him.

—Reflection Questions—

1. Do I find God's revelation of the Ten Commandments to be something that frees me and shows me the way to happiness, or do they seem to me to be a set of rules and prohibitions which limit me? Please describe your experience in faith.

2. Where have I witnessed the power of Jesus' forgiving love in my community?

Moses before the burning bush, Gebhard Fugel, c. 1920

SUFFERING

Anonymous

Jesus "knows suffering" (Is 53:3)...to suffer with Christ... Just as, if the Christian lives, it is no longer (he) who lives, but Christ who lives in (him), so the sufferings are "the sufferings of Christ in him (2 Cor 1:5)" (589).

In Is 53 we meet several major characteristics of Jesus. "He was spurned and avoided by men, a man of suffering, accustomed to infirmity, One of those from whom men hide their faces, spurned and we held him in no esteem." In light of this living truth, the mystery of Christian suffering receives a point of revelation that invites us into a consoling co-creative suffering "with Christ" indwelling, if only we learn to accept that which often seems to be unacceptable in our humanity.

Another way to state this is that Jesus' poverty, his human frailty, lives within us. We are images of Jesus through baptism. Often we disdain or hide in the fear of unbelief from the healing power of trusting that Jesus is with us and within us in distressing disguises. Mother Theresa and her Missionaries of Charity Sisters, as prime examples, teach us and invite us by their witness to see Jesus in the distressing disguises of the poor and in our own frailty and poverty-of-spirit.

True Christian suffering is accompanied by the consolation of knowing in faith that Jesus' presence is with us in the most distressing human frailties that we suffer. Faith speaks within our hearts a word, the Word made flesh who is Love. To taste in faith that we are not alone in our sufferings transforms the sting of loneliness and converts quiet despair into hope.

There is a type of suffering that is self-induced, and this is caused by unbelief in the goodness of Jesus' poverty and frailty within us. It can also be caused by unforgiveness in our interior dispositions toward ourselves if we refuse to trust the truth and beauty of Jesus' poverty and frailty alive within our hearts. Whenever I exercise faith and believe in the truth and beauty of Jesus' presence indwelling in my human frailty, the fruit of loving self-acceptance is tasted. This spiritual sweetness consoles and ennobles our human suffering. It provides good news. Real joy is tasted and it is contagious.

A Personal Witness

During a recent retreat, a time of special solitude and silence for prayer, a good deal of human fright surfaced in my memory around sufferings that had been endured throughout my life. I wanted to avoid, even run from, acknowledging this fright, but there was a clear call to face these realities alive within my memory, and relate all of this to God. It was awkward but I was given the grace to be real and honest in prayer. Able to acknowledge and relate to Jesus some of the memories that included poignant fright, something unusual transpired within my heart. To my surprise I heard a quiet gentle voice, Jesus' voice saying, "I am your fright!" Something strange and beautiful changed in my experience of human fright. My words fall short, but I felt a loving union with Jesus' own humanity, and suddenly the pain of having believed that I was alone in my fright was healed. The belief that something was wrong with my humanity for being frightened was also converted. A new belief in Jesus' own human fright having accompanied me and having suffered within me throughout my life gave me a profound new serenity and confidence in God's sovereign love. A new understanding in faith was supplied. Now, through God's grace, I was able to taste and see the truth and beauty of never having been alone in my frailty and any human fright in the circumstances of my life. I also began to understand a small part of the great mystery of Jesus as the Infant, and what beauty and truth about God's presence at work in my human frailty is revealed through the Christ Child's human frailty. The power of God is made manifest in the glory of human weakness. Not only is it acceptable, this frailty in love is a place, so-to-speak, where beauty saves. It is a place to receive the might and strength of God's glory (cf. 1 Col 10-12)! The healing of aloneness was/is real. I experience fright now within a confidence that Jesus' humanity is abiding within and He is my newfound strength and consolation. Whenever I hear the Scripture passage "I make all things new," (Rev 21:5) my whole being smiles in silent listening as I remember what has transpired. The power of Jesus' love fills me with gratitude.

Conclusion

Christian suffering carries consolation whenever we are able to trust that the presence of Jesus' humanity is suffering with us and within our human frailty and poverty of spirit. Jesus as divine love has "taken upon himself the chastisement that makes us whole...and by his stripes we are healed" (Is 53:5). All praise to Jesus Christ!

—Reflection Questions—

1. Is there anything about my human frailty that I need to accept more in faith?
2. Am I experiencing the presence of Jesus with me in my sufferings?

Smiling Crucified Jesus, Courtesy of Franca Salvo A.O.,
an Apostolic Oblate in the Secular Institute, Pro-Sanctity.

Heaven and Hell

Brent S. Gordon

Heaven is the invisible yet attentive paternal presence that surrounds the world with inexhaustible bounty, even for the birds of the air, both for just and unjust (231).

*Fire and abyss, the wrath of heaven and the opening of the earth, the curse of God and the hostility of creation:
this is hell (234).*

As much as the question of our ultimate destiny, of our eternal state, preoccupies us, this alone does not account for the interest in heaven and hell. Very little of our popular fascination with hell can by genuinely claimed as out of concern for our immortal soul. Interest in heaven is perhaps a bit more direct, though it is worth reflecting on how seldom heaven is seen in our cultural consciousness in relation to hell. For all our interest, however, and whatever the motivations of that interest are, there remains a particular facet which requires our attention: the *pres-*

entness of these places. Not to discount their distinct existence, we must note nevertheless that the realities of heaven and hell are made manifest in creation, in our present moment.

The Invisible Yet Attentive
Paternal Presence: Heaven

The sky, in its vastness and its simultaneous presence and distance, signifies both the presentness and transcendence of heaven and, thus, of God. "God reveals Himself to man through the whole of creation, including its visible structures" (229). Immediately Fr. Léon-Dufour draws our attention to the use of "heaven" throughout Scripture to denote both the sky (and, by extension, the cosmos beyond it) and the abode of God. We must note this at the outset in order to avoid an overly simplistic, surface-level understanding of Scripture; for example, by conflating the sky with heaven and thereby searching for heaven out the window of an airplane. These dual uses of the term are not without purpose, however. "There is the heaven of 'heaven and earth' and the heaven distinct from the earth. But it is more especially the first which enables us to see the second" (229-230).

The sky naturally signifies to us the greatness of God: "Though the depths of the earth and the abyss below are equally inaccessible to man, still the inaccessibility of the sky is continually exposed to him and, as it were, visibly revealed" (230). While it is true that our technological abilities enable us to go ever deeper into the mysteries of our planet (both literally and figuratively), the sky evokes a particular wonder. The sky is open to our vision and our admiration, but it is present while reminding us on the ground of its great distance from us. We *see* how much the sky extends beyond us. This is why the sky becomes a fitting symbol for the heavenly realm of God which is also beyond us.

Still, this is not to imply a total separation as if there were two planes of reality, rather, the relationship is sacramental. "The Bible does not acknowledge two heavens, one physical and the other spiritual. Rather it is in the visible heavens that the Bible discovers the mystery of God and His work" (230). The emphasis on the visible heaven signifying the invisible one reveals an important characteristic of God. To say that God "dwells in" and "rules from" heaven is not meant to imply a separation between God and the world, but rather such phrases "tell of a universe entirely ruled by God's sovereign power and wholly penetrated by His knowledge" (230). When he had finished building the Temple, Solomon indeed prayed: "Is God indeed to dwell on earth? If the heavens and the highest heaven cannot contain you, how much less this house which I have built!" (1Kgs 8:27) And it was right and true what he said, but we must not forget that the glory did indeed come down upon the Temple. This in turn was a foreshadowing of God coming to dwell fully on earth in the Incarnation.

Jesus is the person in whom heaven and earth meet.

"Heaven" is spoken of as a reality intimately connected to the Father by Jesus—Jesus reveals the kingdom of heaven just as he reveals the Father. "Thus heaven becomes a living and triumphant reality; the kingdom of heaven arrives on earth" (231). We note here along with Fr. Léon-Dufour that Jesus' mission "consists in joining together earth and heaven forever; to see to it that the 'kingdom of heaven comes' and that God's will is done 'on earth as it is in heaven' (Matt 6:10)..." (231). When the will of God is effected on earth, the barrier between it and heaven is truly rent away (Col 1:20). Still, we must note the words of St. Paul that "while we are at home in the body we are away from the Lord" (2 Cor 5:8). Heaven is made manifest on earth but is still beyond it. "Heaven will be our new universe, since ours is forever that of Word made flesh and of His body" (232).

The Hostility of Creation: Hell

We should immediately note the effect of Jesus Christ on the reality of hell; that is, on the relationship between the "netherworld" as the abode of the dead and of "hell" as the eternal lot of the unrepentant.

"The netherworld, like hell itself, is the kingdom of death. Without Christ there would be in the world only one hell and one death, the eternal death, that is all powerful. If there is a 'second death' (Rev 21:8), separable from the first, it is because Jesus Christ by His death has broken the reign of death... Jesus

Christ uses [Old Testament images of the netherworld] to describe eternal damnation because they are more than images; they are the *reality of what the world would be without Him*" (233; emphasis added).

In order to understand the revelation of hell presented by Christ, it is therefore necessary to understand something of the historical development of thinking on both death and sin.

Hell was gradually understood by viewing earthly calamities and early deaths. In the ancient Israelite understanding old age leading eventually to death is the common fate of humanity; it is simply the way of things. However, violent deaths or the deaths of those whose "time had not yet come" led to a depiction of Sheol as "like an insatiable monster (Prov 27:20; 30:16) lying in wait for its prey and carrying it away in full vigor." While Sheol, the shadowy realm where all the dead are consigned, was characterized as a devouring beast, it also began to be cast as a force commanding armies. "This invasion of the infernal forces 'into the land of the living' (Isa 38:11) is the tragedy and scandal" (233). We see here how an understanding of the reality of death led to a view of "infernal forces" as enemies of humanity *on earth*.

Linking the realm of the dead to the circumstances of death on earth led to a realization of the link between death and sin. Thus calamity, destruction, and "early" death became connected to the righteous anger of God as punishment for sins. This is seen, and perhaps most widely known, in the story of the destruction of Sodom and Gomorrah: "the Lord rained down sulfur…[and] fire from the Lord out of heaven" (Gen 19:24). Fr. Léon-Dufour directs us to another example regarding "the valley of Gehenna, the place of pleasure which is destined to become a place of horror" (233). Citing the closing lines from the book of Isaiah, Fr. Léon-Dufour brings into stark view the reality of hell: "They shall go out and see the corpses of the people who rebelled against me; for their worm shall not die, their fire shall not be extinguished; and they shall be an abhorrence to all flesh" (Isa 66:24). The fiery punishment of death—hell—is thus known by punishments incurred on earth, and it is the visible manifestation of such events that reveals the distinction between Sheol (death) and hell (Death).

The Lord works through creation in effecting just punishment. This is seen particularly in the Wisdom literature, which often underscores how the Lord rewards the just and punishes the unrepentant sinners—despite initial appearances of the success of the wicked. Especially in the book of Wisdom, we see how creation itself shows the reality of divine punishment. "And while the Lord gives to the just their reward, 'He arms creation for punishing His enemies' (Wis 5:15ff). Hell is no longer localized in the lowest depths of the earth; it is 'the universe let loose against the foolish' (5:20)" (234).

It is from the above understanding that the revelation of the New Testament begins. Here we see the connection. For the "paternal presence" of God throughout and within all creation marks the reality of heaven—and so too, this very creation be-comes foreign and hostile to one who seeks to cut himself off from that presence. When the Lord Jesus speaks of saying to the unrepentant, "I do not know you" (Matt 25:13), we see that His creation then does not know them either. *This* is why we can speak of hell in terms of deep and unrelenting loneliness. Hell is self-imposed abandonment from the Creator and, there-fore, from all creation.

A Personal Witness

Several years ago I worked as a front desk attendant for a parish. In addition to answering phones and doing some basic clerical work, my job consisted of being the "first line of de-fense" between the ladies who worked in the parish office and any of the homeless, under-housed, or mentally unstable people who would come looking for help or to talk to someone. Given that most of these people came in only once—we had very few "regulars"—the women in the office felt more comfortable with having a man present in case of any dangerous situations.

One day a young man walked into the parish office. He looked disheveled, as if he had been sleeping on the streets. His youth was somewhat surprising, as most people who came in asking for help were at least in their forties. He looked at me with very intense eyes in a way that rather unsettled me and asked to speak to a priest. I asked if there was anything in particular he wanted to talk with a priest about, or if it was a private matter (this was a standard question, in case they were just asking for financial help which could be handled by me at the front desk). He responded that it was very important he speak to a priest because he had received a "new gospel." From his pocket he pulled out a very battered iPhone and told me it had come to him there.

I asked him to wait in the lobby and I went down the hall and around the corner to the priest's office. When I knocked he asked me through the door what was needed. I told him that a young man was asking to speak to a priest and, wanting to give him some advance notice added, "This one seems a bit crazy." As I led the priest back around the corner and into the lobby the young man was nowhere to be found. The office manager told us that he had walked out. "And by the way," she said as she turned to me, "your voice carries down the hall."

There are a handful of experiences that, though they seem on one level rather simple, stand out as pivotal in my life. Even though I meant no malice, I felt in the aftermath of this encounter, the realization that this young man heard what I said and left. A sad loneliness shocked me (and continues to do so). I began by thinking how lonely this young man must have felt as he heard what I said, how he left a Catholic church feeling perhaps more alienated than when he had entered. And then I realized that I what I had said led to his feeling that way. The loneliness within my heart spread. In that moment I knew in faith that, in my lack of charity, somehow I had become closed to the poor and the world. In that moment was a glimpse of hell. It is also a great testimony to the mercy of God—to that "invisible yet attentive paternal presence." It was only a glimpse of how easily we can become closed to the world and the poor. I was able to repent. Through Jesus' merciful presence, revealing heaven on earth as the Father's attentive paternal presence loving me, I was able to get back up again and continue to serve. My service was now informed by a new strength and confidence. The Father's love, His attentive heavenly presence, saved me from hellish self enclosure to the poor and the world. Through confession and forgiveness my heart was regenerated in mercy. I actually experienced that the Father brought something good out of what was evil. There is a new informed knowledge of how Jesus saves us through the poor, as well as a new compassion that is God's gift.

Conclusion

For all we talk about them, for all we speculate, and for all we are surrounded by a cultural interest in them, the realities of heaven and hell can be elusive to us. As a people, we can become so fixated on our "final end." This is understandable as we look toward eternity. But, we must never lose sight of the One in whom these realities, in whom all realities, are properly ordered and have their being. We believe in an Incarnate

God and that, as Jesus walked this earth, He revealed mysteries far deeper than some distant metaphysical places. Through the eyes healed by Jesus Christ we can see the very comforting joys of heaven and the very lonely pains of hell made manifest here on this earth, now in this present moment. Let us seek to abide always in the presence of Jesus Christ in whom heaven touches earth.

A Literary Icon[1] as a Conclusion

Once upon a time there was a peasant woman and a very wicked woman she was. And she died and did not leave a single good deed behind. The devils caught her and plunged her into a lake of fire. So her guardian angel stood and wondered what good deed of hers he could remember to tell to God; "She once pulled up an onion in her garden," said he, "and gave it to a beggar woman."

And God answered: "You take that onion then, hold it out to her in the lake, and let her take hold and be pulled out. And if you can pull her out of the lake, let her come to Paradise, but if the onion breaks, then the woman must stay where she is."

The angel ran to the woman and held out the onion to her. "Come," said he, "catch hold and I'll pull you out." And he began cautiously pulling her out. He had just pulled her right

---

1   Fyodor Dostoevsky, *The Brother's Karamazov*, trans. Constance Grant (New York: Dutton, 1927), part III, book VII, ch.3.

out, when the other sinners in the lake, seeing how she was being drawn out, began catching hold of her so as to be pulled out with her.

But she was a very wicked woman and she began kicking them. "I'm to be pulled out, not you. It's my onion, not yours." As soon as she said that, the onion broke.

And the woman fell into the lake and she is burning there to this day.

So the angel wept and went away.

—Reflection Questions—

1. What are my onions, and how having seen a glimpse of heaven, must I work to share that glimpse with others?

2. How is Jesus inviting me to accept, rejoice and abide in the Father's attentive heavenly presence?

Miracles

Moïse Staël Dantes

*It is not uncommon for some Christians to consider the very
notion of miracle as strictly limited, and on the contrary, for
others to show themselves quite fond of false marvels. These
opposed excesses have a common source which is nurtured by
a certain kind of apologetic of long-standing vigor:
in miracles all they see is a defiance of natural laws.
What is overlooked is their role as signs
"adapted to the intelligence of all" (360).*

Years ago, an event that should have been a joyous oc-
casion for a young couple, disintegrated into a juncture for
despair and desolation. During the birth of their first child, it
became very apparent that something had gone wrong during
the pregnancy. The couple had just been thrust into a realm of
uncertainty. With all their options exhausted, the couple could
only hope for a miracle. Would their prayers for the healing of

their child be heard, or would this gift, this manifestation of their love, be snatched away from their imploring hands? Many times we find ourselves in a similar place as this couple. Maybe our situations are not as extreme, but nonetheless in our various situations we desire some sign that God is acting in our lives. In this brief essay, we will explore the biblical understanding of miracles as efficacious signs of God's presence in our midst, as outlined in the *Dictionary of Biblical Theology* by Fr. Xavier Léon-Dufour.

Miracles as Signs in Scripture

While the Old Testament is filled with magnificent occurrences, Fr. Léon-Dufour makes it a point to distinguish "the fictitious marvels of certain books" from the two periods in which we encounter miraculous events: when Moses led the Israelites out of slavery and Joshua led them into the promised land; during the time of Elijah and Elisha, "the restorers of the covenant of Moses" (360). Miracles in the Old Testament are signs of God's activity and revelations to God's people. Their primary function is as "sign" or "symbol." These words are used more commonly than "miracle," emphasizing the dimension of sign and symbol that is embedded in the prophet. "Thus, the person of the prophet can be a sign, for his existence symbolizes the Word of God made known through the actions of the prophet" (362). The prophet's words gain credibility when accompanied by miraculous signs because they reveal concretely the salvation that is being proclaimed. Miraculous deeds proved the authenticity of the prophet. In other words, performing a miracle was proof that you are actually sent by God and not an imposter.

As we enter into the New Testament we see this theme of miracles as sign in the person of Jesus. Jesus showed us that the Messianic Kingdom proclaimed by the prophets is present in Himself by the miracles He performed. In the Old Testament we saw that Miracles were the signs that a prophet was sent by God. Miracles gave legitimacy to the words of a prophet. As such, we encounter an understanding that one cannot separate these signs from the words of the one performing them. The difference between Jesus and the prophets we highlighted in the Old Testament, however, is that Jesus claims to actually be God. This claim points to very significant implications. "The very titles which Jesus gives himself, the power he claims for himself, the salvation he preaches, and the renunciation he demands—all are seen to receive the mark of divine authenticity from his miracles by those who have not rejected the truth of his message from the outset"(363). Thus, for the Christian, Jesus is not just a sign or symbol but the actual presence of God made incarnate in the midst of His people.

Today the Church carries on the mission of Christ. Through the events surrounding Pentecost, the Church received the Holy Spirit and the power to manifest concretely the salvific power of the risen Jesus. We continue to experience miracles through the actions of the Holy Spirit and hold genuine miracles with high esteem. For example, we witness a miracle each time we attend Mass, celebrate the sacraments, or come together in prayer because God is present in all of these events transforming us. The disheartening reality is that we have grown so accustomed to these miracles that we tend to take them for granted. We tend to grow complacent and lose sight of the beauty and power to be found in these moments. Some of us have also witnessed miracles in what we commonly think of as Biblical proportions. When you witness God working in such a big way, you become hyper-aware of God's hand at work in every aspect of your life. I know this because this is what happened to my family and me. The couple from the beginning of this essay are my parents and I am the baby who almost didn't make it.

A Personal Witness

My mother loves to tell the story of my name's origin. I remember how she would proudly proclaim this story at the major celebrations that marked milestones in my life. The story begins when she was six months pregnant with me. She began having dreams where a woman, robed in white, would approach her and tell her she was going to have a boy. The dream told her his name should be a combination of Moïse and Joseph, which would be Moseph. However, my mother did not like the name and put the dream out of her memory. When I was born, I was named Staël George Dantes. In the hours that followed my birth it became evident that there was a problem. When my parents took me to the doctor I was diagnosed with a paralytic colon. This is when there is an obstruction of the intestine due to paralysis of the intestinal muscles resulting in an inability to remove waste from my body on my own. This condition would require me to undergo invasive surgery to correct. The surgery is dangerous and if performed incorrectly would leave permanent damage.

My parents were faced with two impossible choices: raise thousands of dollars to fly me from Haiti, where I was born, to New York in order to ensure a safe procedure; or take a major risk and have the surgery done in Haiti. My mom prayed for an answer and received a message from a friend she hadn't seen or heard from since the sixth grade. The friend informed my mom that a woman, robed in white, came to her in a dream and instructed that my name should be changed to Moïse. My mother remembered the dream she had months ago and was shocked because she never told anyone about that dream. My name was changed to Moïse Staël Dantes and I was healed. All my internal organs were functioning properly without the surgery. The doctors could not explain the change but my parents were certain a miracle had taken place.

After they felt I was old enough, my parents shared the story of my miraculous healing with me. It has become a point of meditation and prayer for me. I started to see all the times that God's hand was actively moving in my life. When I was two years old, my family was forced to leave our home in Haiti and find refuge in the United States. At the time this was a tragedy, as we were ripped away from our extended family and beloved country. However, we realized what a blessing it was when I entered school and it was revealed that I needed extra assistance in class. I would never have received this specialized assistance in Haiti. God would continue to make his presence known to my family by always providing us with exactly what we needed just when we needed it, no matter how small the need was in day-to-day life. Often people tend to miss these tiny miracles. I have since entered the seminary hoping to glorify God through sharing my life and the gift of faith in a God of miracles. With all that I am I hope to minister as a future priest in my diocese. Ever since the day I was healed, my family has become strong believers in the old adage: "God is in the details." I pray that my ministry strengthens people's desire and abilities to see the miracles at work in all of the details of their lives. The Holy Spirit is a God of wonder!

Our world is full of hurt, brokenness, poverty and fear. In these times, it is clear to me that everyone wants to know that someone cares. We pray for the aid of the Almighty to get us through our struggles. We want to know that God walks among us and works wonders in our midst. Miracles are the efficacious signs of God's presence in our lives. They are everywhere for those who have eyes of faith and who seek Him in the details of everyday life. We often do not seek the presence of the risen Jesus in the small things because of some self-will or fear that needs to be surrendered to believing in His great love and the might of His glory alive. The miracle of the risen Jesus' love and mercy serve as reminders that point us to new intimacy with the Blessed Trinity who is indwelling through the gift of baptism. Remembering what God has done in our lives keeps us close to Jesus' Spirit and helps us to see the miracle of the Father's providential care in daily events. The miracles that He desires to continue to lavish upon us through the sacraments and in so many other ways promise a future full of hope and joy (Jer 31:1-6).

—Reflection Questions—

1. In what ways have I experienced miracles in my life and how does this serve as a reminder for me of the Father's providential love?
2. What prevents me from being attentive to Jesus' Spirit at work in my own life?

Blessing and Curse

Anonymous

To bless is to speak a creative and vivifying gift whether prior to its being produced under the form of a prayer, or whether after the event under the form of thanksgiving (48).

The Lord said to Moses: Speak to Aaron and his sons and tell them: This is how you shall bless the Israelites. Say to them:
The Lord bless you and keep you!
The Lord let his face shine upon you, and be gracious to you!
The Lord look upon you kindly and give you peace!
So shall they invoke my name upon the Israelites, and I will bless them.

~ Num 6:22-27

This blessing, known in our Jewish heritage as the Priestly Blessing, is one of the simplest and best-known of all blessings in the Jewish tradition. Traditionally given by *kohanim* (Hebrew priests, particularly Levites), it has been adopted as a frequent and popular blessing given before bed, before a long journey, and before the Sabbath from parents for their children. We have welcomed this blessing into our own Christian tradition as well: it is used as one of the Solemn Blessings at the conclusion of the Mass, and is echoed in the final words of Morning and Evening Prayer: "May the Lord bless us, protect us from all evil, and bring us to everlasting life."[1] Does this *mean* anything to us? Isn't it natural that this would stir up in us some sense of a powerful gift being conferred, and gratitude toward what is promised to come? Blessing is the speaking of one's desire for God to generously pour out his love upon the one being blessed. *Blessing is a verbal act of love.*

The Words of Spirit and Life

Perhaps because of how commonplace blessings are, we often dismiss them as formulaic, reduce them to pietistic remarks, or lose sight of their purpose within religious ritual (47). As a result, we forget the very words we say—and the life-giving grace which seeks to burst through them. The power of blessing

---

1   Older versions use the word "keep" instead of protect, making the parallels even clearer.

is in its being spoken. A blessing conveys quite literally, in the Greek *eulogia* and in the Latin *benedictio*, the effect of "speaking the good." If we only knew the tremendous power behind our words and at work in our words! "Blessing is word as much as gift, *speaking* as much as *good*...because the good which it carries with it is not a precise object, a definite gift; because it belongs not to the sphere of *having* but of *being*; and because it stresses not the action of man but the creation of God" (48).

Of equal interest is the original Hebrew word *beraka*, which is connected to kneeling and adoration (48), implying a sense of awe and reverence before the goodness of God. Perhaps it is for this reason that the most frequent and exuberant form of blessing in the Bible is the proclamation: "Blessed be...!"[2] These cries of praise typically come *after* the gift has been received, where it is an act of thanksgiving. It is a universal praise of the goodness of God in all His gifts, deeds, and chosen ones:

> Blessed be [Abraham] by God Most High, the creator of heaven and earth; and blessed be God Most High, who delivered your foes into your hands!
>
> ...
>
> Blessed is the Lord, the God of Israel, who sent you to meet me today! Blessed is your good judgment

---

2   The word for "blessed" in this case is the participle form of the root, *baruk*.

and blessed are you yourself. Today you have prevented me from shedding blood and rescuing myself with my own hand!

…

Blessed be the name of the Lord!

…

Blessed are you, O Lord, the God of our ancestors, praiseworthy and exalted above all forever; and blessed is your holy and glorious name, praiseworthy and exalted above all for all ages!

…

Blessed are you among women!

…

Blessed be the Lord, the God of Israel!

…

Blessed are you, Simon son of Jonah!

…

Blessed are those who have been called to the wedding feast of the Lamb![3]

Blessing is born of an encounter with the mystery of God's goodness. It is a spoken act of love, born of confidence in the generosity of God. "Blessing is a gift which touches life and its mystery, and it is a gift expressed by the word and its mystery" (48).

---

3   See, respectively, Gen 14:19-20; 1 Sam 25:32-33; Ps 113:2; Dan 3:52; Luke 1:42; Luke 1:68; Matt 16:17; Rev 19:9.

The Words of Death and Judgment

The nature of blessing is also revealed in its antithesis: curse. If blessing is a verbal act of love through which God grants life and grace; cursing, at its core, is a terrible thing indeed: "Through the power of the spoken word... the curse calls forth the dreaded power of evil and sin, the inexorable logic which leads from evil to misfortune" (106). Whereas a blessing is a free gift, a curse is a consequence—"if/because you do X, you will be cursed." A curse is a declaration of punishment, woe, and even perdition, rendered against those who bring about evil; all curses trace their roots back to the seedbed of Original Sin.

Like blessings, curses generally come in two varieties: those which seek to maliciously urge sin and suffering further into the world "before the fact," and those which call down punishment on sin and suffering already manifest. Moments of cursing by God and His servants in the Old Testament are always of the second case, and thus are always acts of divine punishment. For example, God curses Egypt with the plagues; the prophets call down curses on sinful Israel to avenge the orphan, the widow, and all the poor; transgressors of the Law will be cursed. Above all of these examples stands the curse of Original Sin, which subsumes all of humanity under its dreadful power.

Christ: Blessing of the Father, Conqueror of the Curse

It is into this sad tragic scene that the fullness of God's blessing, the Word of God Himself, enters and redeems us. Jesus is the Word of blessing from the Father: all of His existence reveals the unfathomable riches of the Father's grace and mercy, which triumphs even "over judgment" (Jas 2:13). Before, God told Abraham: "I will bless those who bless you and curse those who curse you" (Gen 12:3). Now, Jesus commands his disciples to "bless those who curse you" (Luke 6:28). Christ, as the full revelation of the Father's blessing, curses nobody. There is no longer any need to curse: in Christ, the power of the curse has been undone.

Nowhere is this more clear than in the living mystery of Jesus' Cross and Resurrection. The Paschal Mystery is God's supreme declaration of blessing, a blessing so powerful that the most vicious and destructive of all curses—death itself—cannot overtake it. The gift of God's love in the Word made flesh is greater than any evil. By the Paschal Mystery, Jesus Christ conquers the deadly power of the curse, though its presence remains until Jesus Christ proclaims the final judgment, the final banishment of the curse: "Out!"[4]

---

4   See Rev 22:15: "Outside are the dogs, the sorcerers, the unchaste, the murderers, the idol-worshippers, and all who love and practice deceit." See also Léon-Dufour, 108.

A Personal Witness

One of the greatest experiences of blessing in my life began as one of the most awkward. In the months before entering seminary, I started slowly breaking the news of deciding to begin seminary to friends and family. Among these people was my grandfather. My grandfather had a heart of gold and loved his family more than his very life. However, due to an unfortunate experience in his younger years, he was also a fallen-away Catholic. My dad wanted me to call him, to give him the news myself. I think my dad wanted to know both of us had my grandfather's blessing. Giving him the news was terribly awkward, though he took it well. After letting me know I could always change my mind, he said very sincerely: "I love you. I'll be proud of you no matter what you do." Although he didn't say it outright, I knew he was giving me his blessing. That would be one of the last conversations I had with my grandfather. After I left for seminary, there was a deep ache in my heart to share everything with him. Many things happened in those few short months that followed. After over a decade of cancer, the disease finally claimed my grandfather's life, though not before at last making peace with the Church. When I went to his funeral, I remember standing before him, wishing I could speak to him one more time. As I stood there, I felt this immense consolation in the midst of the sorrow, and a voice seemed to say in my heart: "I am so proud of you. I love you." Somehow, I knew it was my grandfather giving me his blessing one last time. I look forward to the day we can pick up where we left off, but until then I am resting in a new depth of peace in the knowledge that I will always have my grandfather's blessing.

Conclusion

Looking for moments of blessing in life is a difficult process to describe. One might say it's like standing in a forest and drinking it in. At first, you see nothing but trees, boring trees. The longer you look, however, the more you notice the sunlight filtering through the branches, the wind rustling each leaf in a different way, the animals darting to and fro, or the faint sound of water. Sometimes blessings feel very straightforward to us —just "boring trees"—but if we stop for just a moment or two and let Jesus' risen love reinterpret the world, we'll notice the incredible truth: God is *constantly* blessing us.

When I look for moments of blessing, I can think of many. But, in the end they all tell the same truth, like a single idea expressed in a hundred synonyms, or different notes of the same chord: everywhere I look, the Father is blessing me, laboring to love me in new and creative ways. In that moment, I look into the Heart of Jesus, silently burning, and I realize... "Yes, I am blessed." What else can I do but give thanks?

—Reflection Questions—

1. When was there a moment in my life where I knew that I was blessed? What did "blessing" mean to me in that moment?

2. Reflecting on how "blessing" means "speaking the good," how do I bless others in everyday life? How do others bless me?

JUDGMENT

Christopher Awiliba

Our confidence in the day of judgment (1 John 4:17)
comes from God's love for us already manifested in
Christ, so that we have nothing to fear (281).

Fr. Léon-Dufour, in the *Dictionary of Biblical Theology*, traces the history and meaning of judgment from the Old to the New Testament. He starts this history by affirming that, "faith in the judgment of God is never put in doubt" (278). Our understanding of God's judgment, in this contemporary and secular world, often imbues a sense of fear in us. This fear often raises questions in our minds as to why God would "condemn" His own creation, which He created out of love. The point I want to focus on is the fear that surrounds the judgment of God. Our fear should lead us to a personal and committed relationship with God. Fear of judgment should be a chaste fear that St. Augustine speaks of in his writings. Also, judgment is a call to holiness because it is a manifestation of the love and justice of God. Seeing the judgment of God in this regard will dispel the terror that often surrounds our hearts, and will bring us to a true love of the judgment of God.

Judgment is an embodiment of God's love, a call to holiness and a call to repentance and conversion. St Augustine in his sermon on the First Letter of John explained that:

> When we begin to desire what is good, there will be a chaste fear in us. The fear by which we fear being cast into hell with the devil is not yet chaste, since it does not come from the love of God but from the fear of punishment. But when you fear God in the sense that you do not wish to lose him, you embrace him and you desire to enjoy him.[1]

Out of His infinite love, God reveals Himself to humanity in order to draw all men to Himself. Christ said, "When I am lifted up from the earth I will draw all men to myself" (John 12:32). By this action of grace, the soul that was distanced from Christ is now brought to a relationship of love and trust in Him. Christ, out of love, gives himself for all men to bring them to the Father. This is our confidence and hope in the judgment of God.

---

1 Augustine, "Homilies on First John." Translated by H. Browne. From *Nicene and Post-Nicene Fathers, First Series*, Vol. 7 (1888; New Advent, 2009), edited by Kevin Knight. http://www.newadvent.org/fathers/1702.htm

Judgment is also a call to conversion and repentance. Léon-Dufour states that: "Apostolic preaching as found in the discourses from Acts of the Apostles to the Book of Revelation concurs giving an essential place to the proclamation of the judgment with its summons to conversion" (280). "On the day of wrath the just judgment will be revealed (Rom 2:5). It is impossible to flee (Rom 2:3) because God will judge even the hidden actions of men (Rom 2:6; 1 Cor 4:4)" (281). This brings to heart the sovereign power of God. God knows all hearts and thoughts, and nothing can be hidden from Him. It is when we try to hide things from God we miss out on the love that comes with His judgment. Hiding leads to unchaste fear and insecurity.

The love that clouds the judgment of God calls us to holiness and brings us to salvation. Fr. Léon-Dufour explains this, using excerpts from St. Paul's letter to the Romans:

Since the day that sin entered the world through the first man, all men have been judged worthy of condemnation (Rom 5: 16-18). No one can escape by his own merits. But when Jesus, the son of God became flesh, died as a result of our sins, God condemned the sin of the flesh to free us from its yoke (Rom 8:3). Now is the justice of God revealed, not the justice which punishes but the justice which brings justification and salvation (Rom 3:21). All men deserve judgment, but all are gratuitously justified if only they believe in Jesus Christ (Rom 3:24) (281).

A Personal Witness

Growing up in a multicultural society in Ghana with different ideologies and practices, I realized that I only behaved well out of fear of punishment. I had the notion that God is a God of justice who punishes sins without delay. This gave me an image of a fearsome God who is always on the alert to punish "perpetrators." I only chose to do good because of the fear of judgment. I thought it was all about me.

Experiencing God's love gave me an entirely different attitude toward judgment. The unhealthy fear of being punished was now turned to a chaste fear as described by St. Augustine. I experienced this love through the Sacrament of Reconciliation. I realized that God is always calling me to Himself in the midst of my weaknesses and sins. God, through His love, wishes to bring all humanity to Himself. I am created out of God's love, and I respond to His love by building a personal and committed relationship with Him. Realizing this dispelled the fear of punishment I had, and brought me to an intimate relationship with God. I always thank God for bringing me to this new understanding about the love that surrounds His judgment. I am ever grateful for being able to taste and see in my own life what St. Augustine writes for us to learn and appropriate in our Christian faith.

Conclusion

It is especially important that we realize that "our confidence in the day of judgment (1 John 4:17) comes from God's love for us already manifested in Christ, so that we have nothing to fear" (281). The threat now weighs only upon evil men; people who neither desire to love God nor fear His judgment. Jesus has come to deliver us from judgment. We should have a chaste fear of knowing that our sins prevent us from embracing the love of God manifested through His Son Jesus Christ. The Act of Contrition is a prayer that gives me confidence in God's judgment and is one that is always filled with consolation and mercy. Mercy triumphs over judgment! May the risen Jesus draw me and all of us evermore into His intimate love. Pray with me now the Act of Contrition:

> O my God, I am heartily sorry for having offended you, and I detest all my sins, because I dread the loss of heaven and the pains of hell; but most of all because they offend you, my God, who are all good and deserving of all my love. I firmly resolve, with the help of your grace, to confess my sins, to do penance, and to amend my life. Amen.

—Reflection Questions—

1. What are some areas in my life where I experience fear of being judged?
2. How can I further receive a true chaste fear, a fear of isolating myself from receiving the risen Jesus' judgment, always a judgment of consoling love and mercy?

AUTHORITY AND POWER

Thomas Coppola

> *God inaugurates in the history of His people*
> *a plan of salvation in which earthly authority*
> *is going to take on a new meaning within the*
> *perspective of the redemption (37).*

The God of Israel presents Himself through authority over and against creation and through the power of salvation by faith. As we read in the Scriptures, the religiosity of Israel matures and eventually recognizes God's power not only voiced through natural forces or social liberation, but also through the spiritual deliverance from sin, which comes from the love of the all-powerful God. Authority is firstly understood by the Israelites through its association with domination. Secondly, it is personalized in salvation through faith, and thirdly it is radically refigured by Christ as a mode of service for all men in charity.

We find in Scripture a new interpretation for authority in

Christ Jesus: "The Son of Man did not come to be served but to serve" (Matt 20:28). The Lord of all Creation, Christ Jesus, who has authority to speak storms into calm, teaches a new understanding of authority, not as a power for oneself but as a *service for others*.

Authority and Power as Domination

Creation is the primal circumstance of God's omnipotence. Out of nothing, He creates; out of chaos, He brings order. By His Word, the heavens and the earth were made; by His breath, man was given life. Power is displayed by the God Who can "do whatever he wills" (Ps 115) and to whom "nothing will be impossible" (Luke 1:37). Both over and against creation, as well as through creation's order, God manifests His omnipotence, since "by His power mountains leap or melt away," and since He in fact "determined this order" (439).

His authority, like the authority of countless men in the Hebrew Scriptures (e.g., King David, Josiah, Nebuchadnezzar, Cyrus, etc.), is an exercise of dominion. This theme of authority over and against something is visible in the ancient rulers. Throughout the Hebrew Scriptures we see leaders establish law and order, conquer foreign nations, and subject peoples under them. Authority is identified with power, and its influence channels down from the highest principality and is felt by the lowest class.

Authority and Power as Salvation

A turning point occurs for Israel when the power of God is realized not so much in the success of its army or in the fortification of Jerusalem, but in the personal life of one with faith. Faith illumines the mind and heart of the Israelites to experience *personally* the inner operations of God's omnipotence: to give strength to the weak, endurance to the afflicted, and wisdom to the simple. When Israel's acknowledgment of God's omnipotence dares to reach beyond the fathomable workings of nature into the unfathomable workings of grace in faith, which "no eye [has] ever seen" (Isa 64:3), Israel begins to glimpse the beauty of God's hidden power.

Salvation is power *par excellence,* and God fully manifests this hidden power to the one who has allowed his heart and mind to be unlocked to Him. Fr. Léon-Dufour writes, "By faith man opens himself to the power of salvation in the gospel" (442). Herein God's authority reaches its climactic expression. As a greater revelation of power than the magnificence of creation or the violent domination of earthly rulers, the gift of salvation shows the gentle entry of God's love into life. Faith is that key that unlocks the heart and mind to the beauty of power in salvation.

New Meaning of Authority and Power in Christ

Fr. Léon-Dufour writes that "God inaugurates in the history of His people a plan of salvation in which earthly authority is going to take on a new meaning within the perspective of the redemption" (37). Christ inverted the world order: he has made authority into service and salvation into an inner reality, not a political project. Domination has been ousted and salvation by violence is eradicated.

Christ institutes true power and true authority by loving service and passes this reality on to His disciples. In His address to the Apostles, Christ offers the proper orientation for authority: "You know that the rulers of the Gentiles lord it over them, and the great ones make their authority over them felt. But it shall not be so among you. Rather, whoever wishes to be great among you shall be your servant" (Matt 20:25-26). Jesus gives authority its proper direction as a *service*. Since God has served Israel in salvation, so too should the Apostles serve others.

The commandment that Jesus gives on authority is not something distant, but is a reenactment of the grace received in salvation. Disciples of Christ are participating in what Christ has done and is doing for them. Salvation is service in and with Christ Jesus' risen presence. Granting salvation is also the greatest exercise of authority and power. Jesus manifests the unity of true authority and true service in the power of love.

A Personal Witness: The Authority and Power of God's Salvation in the Living Word

God's service toward us who believe is operative and effective in everyday faith. Jesus' risen presence serves men through His Word, which grants the joy and consolation that human hearts desire. To experience Jesus Christ's voice in the loving, personal Word of Scripture is to experience participating in the saving love of Jesus Christ. Salvation is power *par excellence*, and so an on-going experience in faith of the Word addressing our hearts is an encounter with the authority and power of God. His Word is full of the power of Jesus' Spirit.

A personal experience related to this began during 2015 in my second year at seminary. After reading *Verbum Domini* by Pope Emeritus Benedict XVI before the Blessed Sacrament, and coming into a profound awe of Scripture, I began to see the *power* of the Word of God to fight evil. This battle with evil can constantly drain our joy and hope in the midst of our daily living. The eyes of my heart were opened to see the living effects of the Word as God addresses our hearts. Jesus' Spirit was and is tasted and seen to be at work in us who believe, and these effects are real, practical, and salvific.

Unconsciously we accept false teachings each day and soak into our minds lies about our humanity through the media and through our worldly interactions. But, by constancy in prayer allowing the living Word of God to penetrate our hearts, evil lies are experienced as corrected and a new, right-ordered love for our humanity transpires. Soaking in the living Word gives joy and peace. One example of this type of grace in my life is when the line in Psalm 62 from Evening Prayer of the Liturgy of the Hours stood out as addressing my heart: "My soul rests in God alone." After deriving deep consolation from receiving this verse as I prayed, I continued to reflect on this line over the course of that day. And, on the next day, I found myself desiring to live throughout the day repeating the verse slowly again and again. Through that practice, the Lord opened up for me a simple and clear grace. A single thought immediately occurred to me: my attachment to discovering God's will had become for me a god, an idol. My "effort" to discern God's will had robbed me of much of my prayer life, and my encounter with God in the Scriptures had been diluted to an impersonal quest for His will. My "efforts" had become the center of trying to discover God's will! Self-determination and self-assertion had replaced my vulnerable receptivity to the loving power of the living Word.

I slowly drifted from personally asking God about His will in prayer to impersonally asking myself *about* Him, constantly. I made simple discernments: How much should I offer to God of my finances, possessions, etc.? Where is God in all this? Where is God in my suffering? But, the end of this search was not peace or any real answer. Only worry and anxiety accompanied these efforts and this manner of proceeding in what

I thought was a relationship with God. The answers seemed to grow further away, and I constantly groped in confusion throughout the day. I lived in a cloudy vision filled with anxiety. The God of my heart had morphed in my own head to a far-off, impersonal Deity that ordained good things from above. I was treating the living power of Jesus' Spirit in the living Word as if God were distant. The string connecting my heart and my mind was severed like the ground from the sky, and the God of my mind was isolated from my heart, as if dangling somewhere above me.

The power to see this lie and the power to grow in freedom from the anxiety of trying to become pleasing to such a God did not seem to be in my grasp. I walked blindly. The empty lie weighed heavily on me though, and I felt powerless, unable to lift the heavy burden that broke down my strength and held a grip over my mind. I could not see the specific lie and knew not why my joy had escaped me.

Only in that simple verse from Psalm 62, "My soul rests in God alone," could I experience God's saving power for me through faith. Faith in that Scriptural verse was/is God serving me in His authority and power. It was a service bestowing saving grace. It still breaks into my soul, my heart in everyday life. The nearness of the loving power of Jesus' Spirit in the living Word breaking into my life is so real. I experienced His true authority through His love for me and from an in-breaking grace within. As I prayed, my faith blossomed; as my faith blossomed, my hope increased; as my hope increased, joy entered in; and as joy entered in, I found my God again. That personal power of salvation in the Word is known only to those who believe in the truth of Scripture. I have, through no merit of my own, encountered that truth and I allow myself to be renewed by the Word every day. Each day I now feel led to carry a single verse of Scripture within my heart. I give myself over to God's working through the Word. Personally and prayerfully I am led to dialogue with God throughout the day. Through allowing myself to receive the love present in the Word I experience His power to correct my thinking, and offer consolation to others. The Word's loving power draws me deeper into His holiness, which is His work in me and for me. The focus is not on "my effort" to be pleasing to Him. I am already baptized and through baptism His favor is upon me and the Father's delight is with me. I need not chase a blessing that is already mine to receive more of in daily encounters with the living Word. The power of the Word of God is its ability to search our hearts and minds and reveal to us the truth about ourselves in and through Jesus' risen love. May we stand in awe and adore in praise and thanksgiving the truth we hear in Hebrews 1:1-3, "In times past, God spoke in partial and various ways to our ancestors through the prophets; in these last days, he spoke to us through a son, whom he made heir of all things and through whom he created the universe, who is the refulgence of his glory, the very imprint of his being, and who sustains all things by his mighty Word."

Conclusion

Authority and power were once esteemed as domination. The Hebrew Scriptures are replete with examples of God's domination over and against nature and also through nature: He causes the waters to congeal in the midst of the sea and also shows His magnificence through the terrifying storms. Kings and leaders also exercised power in this fashion. But the ultimate sign of God's power became evident through God's gift of deliverance from sin—that is, through salvation. The Israelites, in faith, eventually saw God's most exalted form of power through deliverance from the tyranny of sin. This was the progression of authority and power as seen in the Hebrew Scriptures.

As Christ entered the world and transcended all human apprehension, He offered a new form of power: authority as service. Those who were in power should not lord it over the others, but be the least among them and be servants of all. In the service of salvation, Christ shows us the supreme example of what true authority and power consists of: loving service toward men. My example has shown the continued service of Jesus Christ, addressing us through His powerful presence in the living Word of Scripture. Its power to heal, comfort, and save is inestimable. I have personally experienced God's loving and personal salvation through the power of the Word in my daily, ordinary life of faith. I pray and hope that you may share with me, ever more fully, this same healing comfort and joy!

—Reflection Questions—

1. How have I experienced the power of the Word of God at work in my daily life?
2. How do I integrate the power of God's healing love in my work environment?

DESIRE AND DISCIPLESHIP: A RELATIONSHIP OF CALL & RESPONSE

Raymond Herard

> *To become His disciple, intellectual or even moral*
> *aptitudes were not important. What matters is a*
> *call, the initiative of which comes from Jesus. To*
> *follow Jesus is to sever with the past, with a com-*
> *plete break if it is a question of privileged disciples*
> *(126).*

To hear Jesus say one's name preceding the invitation "follow me" is one of the rare moments when a human being, content with the everydayness of life, is suspended in reality; caught up and embraced by the wind that flows forth from the Word of God. In that moment, one's life is forever changed by this call to discipleship. Receiving a call requires a response from one's desires. It is in this relationship of *call and response* that a disciple is formed.

The Call and Response of Adam and Eve (Gen 2-3)

God created Adam giving him many gifts. He had one order, not to eat from the tree of knowledge, revealing the tension of good and evil (cf. Gen 2:15). Eve also received this order, which can be seen in her response to the serpent (cf. Gen 3:2-3). This call, brought forth from God to be in paradise, requires a response for love to flourish. Discipleship, in its infancy, is an initial response of the loved to the lover. How do Adam and Eve respond? By disobeying God, in taking God's free gift *of* themselves, *for* themselves. St. Augustine says, "The first evil, then, is this: when man is pleased with himself, as if he were himself light … [t]his evil came first, in secret, and its result was the evil that was committed in the open."[1] This interior movement, also known as desire, draws one to respond. The root of all desire is to live a full, expansive life (123). Adam and Eve's response was to take charge of their own life and push God to the side. In a way saying to God, "I can do this on my own. You put me in charge of all the birds, the animals, the plants, I got it from here." But what happens? They become overwhelmed; the serpent, representing a pull of desire, sends waves through their soul. Instead of calling out to God recognizing their utter

---

1   St. Augustine, *The City of God,* vol. 7: book 14.13, trans. William Babcock (Hyde Park, New York City Press, 2003), 120; It is noted in the text that this notion is also found in Origen, *On Prayer* 29, 18.

dependence, they drowned in the interior storms of their disordered desires, opening a space in the heart that was meant for God to dwell by invitation from the person. God was waiting for them to realize the pull was a call to know, love and serve Him in freedom! A call to recognize themselves at the deepest depth of who they are. By turning their back on God, Adam and Eve pervert their very being. Thus, man becomes ravished with "savage desire" (124). This savage desire is seen throughout the Old Testament scriptures: David and Bathsheba (cf. 2 Sam 11:2f), Ahab and the Vineyard of Naboth (cf. 1 Kgs 21f), just to name a few.

The Call and Response of the Disciples[2]

God's original call to communion was not received well by Adam and Eve. A restoration was needed in order to bring humanity back to God. This restoration can be seen in *The Gospel According to Matthew*, 8:23-27. At this point, Jesus' disciples answered the call and followed. They saw Him work miracles, curing the sick, speak about heaven, and preach the Beatitudes. They are sold! The disciples know with all of their *physical senses* that Jesus is God and they want in on His mission. This is similar to God showing Adam all of what is his

---

2   The idea of calming the interior storms originally comes from Erasmo Leiva-Merikakis in his three volume work, *Fire of Mercy, Heart of the Word: Meditations on the Gospel according to Saint Matthew,* vol. 1 (San Francisco: Ignatius Press, 1996), 360-377.

in paradise (cf. Gen 2:19-20). But something lurks inside the disciples, the *savage desire* passed down from their ancestors. That space in the heart has been filled with disordered desire, with fears, and anxieties. They have not yet responded from the depths of their hearts. Jesus leads them out to the sea, to a violent storm where the boat was swamped by waves (cf. Matt 8:24). He was silently present similar to when God was silently present as Eve gazed upon the fruit. Do the disciples respond like Adam and Eve, by turning back? No, they cry out, "Lord, save us! We are perishing" (Matt 8:25). In their response, they recognize their utter dependence on God, who calms the storm of their savage desires.

A Personal Witness

I am afraid of many things—heights, spiders, complete darkness in small enclosed spaces, to name the top three. The Lord is not concerned with surface fears such as these. It is true; He is with us in those fears. Think of when God made clothes for Adam and Eve before sending them on their way (cf. Gen 3:21). The Lord is concerned and caring about the small details of our lives, but the Lord wants to reign in our hearts. He desires to reign in the areas where there are holes, where our deepest fears and insecurities dwell. He is concerned with the deepest fears that choke our desire to follow Him with our whole heart. Some of those fears are the fear of being alone, of not being loved, or losing control of one's life, and death, just to name a few. The Lord wants all of these fears removed and transformed. We, no matter how hard we try, can not eliminate those fears on our own. To help us, God allows for an interior storm to be brewed within the depths of the soul. This interior storm brings all of these fears to the surface. It is when these fears make their presence known that we can face them and grow in the courage to cry out to the Lord, "Save me! I can not do this on my own!"

Throughout my life I have been conditioned to be an independent person, to rely on myself. I grew in the notion of, "If you can't do it, then I'll do it myself," or the idea, "If you want something done right then you have to do it yourself." This breeds the very fears that take up space in the heart that is meant for God to dwell with His peace and light. "Doing it myself," breeds being alone, not being loved, and losing control of being able to rest in basic goodness that is all around us in God's creation. This "doing it alone" leads to isolating the heart from others and closing in on one's self. This closure can remain indiscernible until we allow ourselves to listen for God's call and voice in daily life.

I first answered in a similar way as the disciples answered Jesus in the Scriptures. I answered on a surface level. I thought to myself, "OK, but what about going back to school or praying every day; come on, that is a lot of prayer. After a week of daily prayer, I won't have much to say to God." Even with all of the "what about" questions, I dropped my net and followed (cf. Matt 4:20). Actually, I dragged my net (my previous life) with me for a few hundred feet until the "storm" of being left behind drew out my desire to let the net go. Being in formation for the sacred priesthood has brought on a massive interior storm, but it is within this storm that my deepest fears are being confronted. I am learning to walk in a boat that is being thrown about by waves; growing in my desire to call on the Lord for help when the fury of the storm approaches. Most importantly, I am learning to sit and rest beside Him within the storm, recognizing my utter dependance on His ability to bring peace to the soul and repair the heart that has been thrown about with savage desires.

To be a disciple is to recognize one's complete and total dependence on God and to follow unreservedly as best as we can follow with generosity. It is important to identify the interior movements of the soul that flow from Jesus' Spirit and those that flow from our fears. In listening and responding to His voice one will choose to respond to Jesus calling your name. His love is freely given. Our response also needs to be a response that is freely returned. With this in mind, through everyday listening and following as a disciple, we become attached to Jesus Christ and destined for eternal life. This whole process of recognition, loving and the calling-out of our name, is a school of learning in discernment how to be interiorly present with Jesus as a person dwelling in our hearts. Adam and

Eve relied on God's physical presence. When God sat back to see if they would recognize Him within themselves, they failed. When the disciples called out to the Lord, He calmed their storm. From that point on the disciples no longer relied on His physical presence. The disciples learn to live in a new adventure. They begin to listen for the Spirit's voice within their hearts. It is a new way of living and being. Now Jesus is preparing them to receive the same Spirit who is guiding Him. "I have told you this while I am with you. The Advocate, the Holy Spirit that the Father will send in my name— he will teach you everything and remind you of all that I have told you. Peace I leave with you; my peace I give to you" (John 14:25-27). My fears are being calmed as I cry out to Jesus and as I learn to listen for that same Spirit that was guiding Him. Of course I need to surrender my fears and follow as a discipleship in trust and in generosity. But I am amazed at how the Spirit delights in teaching us and guiding us. The Spirit dwells with our hearts to calm the interior storms that rob us of being with and always resting in Jesus' presence. He is our peace! I have so much to learn, but life as a disciple is a glorious adventure. I am so grateful to have heard Jesus call my name!

—Reflection Questions—

1. Have I experienced Jesus calling me by name, stirring up a desire to follow as His disciple?
2. In what area(s) of my life do I need to admit that I am in need to begin crying out to the Lord for His help?

Christ in the Storm on the Sea of Galilee,
Rembrandt van Rijn, 1633

THE MISSION

Mission Bethlehem sponsors a center to serve the poor on one of the most destitute sections of Haiti. The name of the mission is Zanj Makenson, a mission with a school and care for malnourished children. As always, we still work with the teachers and children in evangelization, apostolate, catechesis, and meditation on the Word of God. This allows us to serve the poor in social and spiritual ways. The mission is always to the poor, as the poor and for the poor.

Seminarian Authors—First year Theology—
St. Vincent De Paul Regional Seminary

BIOGRAPHIES

ALEXANDER J. SANCHEZ RIVERA is a seminarian for the Diocese of St. Augustine, Florida. He spent his childhood in Philadelphia and his teenage years in Orange Park, Florida, where he finished highschool and worked until deciding to discern the call to priesthood in seminary.

BRENT S. GORDON is a seminarian for the Diocese of Pensacola-Tallahassee, Florida. He was baptized at the age of 22 and is amazed at the merciful love of God.

CHRISTOPHER AWILIBA is from Ghana and currently studying for the Diocese of Savannah, Georgia. He studied Statistics before entering seminary, and completed his philosophical studies in Ghana. He has a passion for evangelization and a desire to share with others his experience and encounter with Christ.

EMMANUEL KYERE ANTWI is a seminarian studying for the Diocese of Savannah, Georgia. He hopes that his essay will encourage the reader to have confidence in God's love and mercy on his/her spiritual journey.

JEREMY LULLY is studying for the Archdiocese of Miami. He grew up in the city of Fort Lauderdale, Florida. Before entering seminary, he attended Florida Atlantic University, earning a Bachelor's degree in Urban Planning. Jeremy enjoys leisure bike rides and Coffee with Jesus comics.

JOHN ARMON S. ANTOLIN was born and raised in Jacksonville, Florida. He is a young man from a Filipino background who likes simple things whose been trying to do his best in life with God's grace to be happy, healthy and holy.

LEO SIQUEIRA was born and raised in Brazil. He is studying for the Archdiocese of Miami. Before entering the seminary, Leo worked with fine woodworking—which is one of his passions.

LOGAN URBAN is a seminarian for the Diocese of Venice, Florida. He enjoys spending time with friends, loves to sing, and is very passionate about the game of ping pong.

MAC HILL was born and raised in Jacksonville Beach, Florida. He is a seminarian for the Diocese of St. Augustine. He enjoys sports, the outdoors, family and friends.

MOÏSE STAËL DANTES is a seminarian studying for the Diocese of Venice in Florida. He was born in Verrettes, Haiti, and moved with his family to the United States when he was 2 years old. Before entering seminary he served in parish youth ministry.

NATHANAEL SOLIVEN is a seminarian for the Diocese of Orlando. Before major seminary, he used to be a language teacher in the Philippines and Spain. Besides classical singing, he loves experiencing other cultures and learning new languages.

PIOTR SAWICKI was born in Gdansk, Poland, in 1988. He came to realize that by rejecting the call to companionship with Jesus he had been building his life on sand, rather than on the rock of Christ's Church. He is studying for the priesthood as a seminarian at Redemptoris Mater Missionary Seminary for the Archdiocese of Miami.

RAYMOND HERARD is studying for the Diocese of Pensacola-Tallahassee. He enjoys journaling, lectio-divina prayer, and learning about discipleship. He is a film enthusiast having studied Film in Los Angeles before entering Seminary.

SAUL ARAUJO is twenty-three years old and originally from Brasília - Brazil. He arrived in the US about five years ago and belongs to the Redemptoris Mater Archdiocesan Missionary Seminary of Miami.

SIMI SAHU is pursuing the Masters in Arts in Theological Studies degree at St. Vincent de Paul Regional Seminary. She is a Certified Public Accountant who worked in various industries before. She received the gift of her faith in Jesus Christ and love for the Holy Catholic Church through the Jesus Youth movement.

BIOGRAPHIES

THOMAS COPPOLA is a 24-year-old Catholic seminarian, studying for the Diocese of Orlando, where he grew up. Before entering seminary, he studied biochemistry and philosophy at the University of Florida. He enjoys reading, running, playing sports (particularly soccer), playing piano and playing guitar.

THOMAS PULICKAL is a seminarian for the Jesus Youth movement and the SyroMalabar Diocese of Chicago. Prior to seminary, he worked as a software developer. His interests are in philosophy, technology, music, and mathematics.

FR. JOHN HORN, S.J., D. Min., serves at St. Vincent De Paul Regional Seminary in Boynton Beach, Florida, as a teacher and spiritual director, specializing in the ministry of the Spiritual Exercises of St. Ignatius of Loyola.

www.ingramcontent.com/pod-product-compliance
Lightning Source LLC
Chambersburg PA
CBHW031845090426
42741CB00005B/364